I Call You Friends

LEADER'S BOOK 2

For post-communion children

Living and Sharing our Faith
A National Project of Catechesis and Religious Education

McCrimmons
Great Wakering, Essex, UK

First published and produced on behalf of
the National Project of Catechesis and Religious Education
in the United in Kingdom in 2010 by
McCRIMMON PUBLISHING CO. LTD
10-12 High Street, Great Wakering, Essex SS3 0EQ
info@mccrimmons.com / www.mccrimmons.com

ISBN 978 0-85597-708-5

Nihil Obstat   Very Revd. Mgr. George Stokes.
Censor Deputatus.

Imprimatur   + Rt. Revd. Thomas McMahon
Bishop of Brentwood.

ACKNOWLEDGEMENTS

I Call You Friends is the result of much dedicated care and many hours of work by diocesan advisers from England and Wales, Our Lady's Catechists and the writers and designers of the multimedia publication *IMFH's Friends*.

Building on the success of the previous programme *Walk With Me, I Call You Friends* takes into account the changing pattern of society and life in the Church today. It was written following a review of National Project publications and a demand for a programme from parishes.

There were some initial meetings of advisers in Birmingham and London. Following that a working group was formed. Heartfelt appreciation and thanks is offered to these writers who met regularly, worked hard and supported each other with prayer, humour and kindness; they were: Sr. Jacqueline Brain, Monika Chmelova, Sr. Nuala Gannon, Sr. Philomena Grimley, Margaret Jones, Diana Klein, Susanne Kowal, Glenys Murch, Rev. Ken O'Riordan, Bridie Stringer and Maggie White. Thanks, too, to Liz O'Brien, who has ensured that the programme meets the requirements of children with special needs. Gratitude is expressed to those dioceses which have actively supported this work.

Thanks to Rev. Gerald Wilson and the community of St Rita's Conference Centre at Honiton for their warm hospitality.

Appreciation is expressed to Bishop Edwin Regan and the Steering Committee of the National Project for their diligent reading of the text, their wise advice, support and encouragement.

The Scripture consultant was Rev. Dr. Adrian Graffy, DSS, STD. PhL.

Victoria Hummell r.a., National Project Co-ordinator

Design and layout by Nick Snode
Typeset in Comic Sans and Calibri

Contents

| Foreword 5

| Introduction 6

| The foundation of *I Call You Friends* 8

| **The Themes** 9-10

| The Word of God:
　　Scripture and tradition 10

| Prayer and Celebration 12

| Preparing for the
　　children's session 14

| The Sessions Overview 15-19

| **The Sessions** 21

　　Autumn Themes 1-3
　　　　Sessions 1 - 9 21

　　Spring Themes 4-6
　　　　Sessions 10 - 18 42

　　Summer Themes 7-9
　　　　Sessions 19 - 27 62

| Resources 82

| Health & Safety 84

| Safeguarding Children 84

Welcome to *I Call You Friends*

Dear Children

I Call You Friends – John 15, 15. Jesus spoke these wonderful words to his disciples on the night before He died out of love for us. He also said that we are his friends if we do what he wishes us to do. Indeed, let us read his own words:

> You are my friends if you do what I command you. I shall not call you servants anymore because a servant does not know his master's business; I call you friends because I have made known to you everything I have learnt from my Father. You did not choose me, no, I chose you!'

As parents or carers who are called to share in the faith development of your children you know how much your child[ren] want to belong. They need to experience the security of loving, strong, and trusting relationships. In this programme, step by step, they are drawn into such a relationship with Jesus, who brings us to the Father through the gift of the Holy Spirit and into communion with all friends. This relationship will grow throughout the journey of their lives as God continues to call them. It is your privilege in these early years to help them listen and respond.

I am very grateful to all who have worked so hard to make this resource available for parish use, especially Sr. Vicky Hummell, the Co-ordinator of the National Project.

I will pray for all those who use *I Call You Friends* – the catechists, the parents and above all the children. I ask God's blessing on you all!

+ Edwin, Bishop of Wrexham
Chairman of the National Project

Introduction

For parents/carers and catechists

The programme *I Call You Friends* offers children the opportunity to know and love God as they learn about and understand their faith. There are three books: Book 1 for children who have not yet made their First Holy Communion; Book 2 for those who have received their First Holy Communion and Book 3 for children over eight years old who are preparing to be received into the Church. Each book is divided into three sections: Autumn, Spring and Summer. Each section has 9 sessions.

Who is it for?

I Call You Friends, Book 2 is for children who have received their First Holy Communion, who are likely to be aged 9 to 11 years old and do not attend a Catholic school.

There is an accompanying 'Activity book' to help the child[ren] deepen their understanding of the sessions. It should be fun and enjoyable. There is no pressure to complete it. It would be good if the child[ren] shared the Activity book with you. You might like to take time to pray and think about the suggestions. It is fine if they have other ideas of what they would like to put in the book.

A prayer for parents

> God, loving Creator, you have given me .....
>   (name your child[ren])
>   to nurture and care for.
> Give me the grace to lead them by example
>   and kind guidance to follow the path of holiness
>   to which they are called.
>
> Help me to listen and understand with patience
>   their cares and concerns,
> so that through the power of the Holy Spirit
>   they may come to know Jesus
>   who calls them His friend.
> Amen.

What about the name?

I Call You Friends[1]. When we consider these words of Jesus from John's Gospel,[2] we remember that we are part of the great mystery of God's loving desire for the whole human family. Throughout the ages, and witnessed again and again in scripture, God continues to call us:

> 'I have called you by your name, you are mine.'[3]

Abraham, who answered God's call to leave his homeland and follow where God led him, is our father in faith and James writing in his letter says:

> 'Abraham believed God and he was called the friend of God.'[4]

Moses was another friend, who listened to God and was close to him. God was pleased with Moses.

> 'The Lord would speak with Moses face to face, just as someone speaks to a friend.'[5]

Jeremiah told the Jewish people who had been deported to Babylon that God was still there with them, caring for them and wanting their good, but they had to want to be friends with Him.

> 'When you search for me you will find me if you seek me with all your heart. I will let you find me says the Lord'[6].

In the person of Jesus, through the Holy Spirit, we are called to closeness with God and to be witnesses and messengers, who bring that call to others.

Parents, carers and catechists who are called to share in the faith formation of young children know that children, in their early years, want above all to belong. They need to experience the security of strong, loving and trusting relationships. In this programme, they are gradually encouraged to develop a friendship with God, who is always faithful to us.

Who is involved?

I Call You Friends affirms parents, who co-operate with God, as the first educators of their children in the ways of faith. In the baptismal rite the blessing of the parents makes it clear that the Church recognises the home as most significant in a child's journey in faith:

---

1. I CALL YOU FRIENDS: Timothy Radcliffe O.P., Continuum International Publishing Group, 2004 ISBN 0826472621, this is also the title of a book for reflection and spiritual insight about living the Gospel in our everyday lives.
2. John 15:15
3. Isaiah 43:1
4. James 2:23
5. Exodus 33:11
6. Jeremiah 29:13-14

Introduction

They *'will be the first teachers of their child in the ways of faith. May they be also the best of teachers, bearing witness to the faith by what they say and do.'* [7]

The first thing the Church asks of the married couple is that they love one another. It is in the family that children first experience human love and from this spring the virtues of faith, hope and charity.

'The family is the community in which, from childhood, one can learn moral values, begin to honour God.' [8]

'The home is the first school of human enrichment.' [9]

The programme calls for the partnership of the family and the parish. It values the role of the parish in catechesis, through its liturgical life, sacramental preparation, Liturgy of the Word with Children and the Christian life of the local Church.

At the beginning of the programme it would be good for catechists to meet with parents/carers to explain how the programme is developed and how they may help at home through the ideas in the Activity book. Some parents may be willing to help with the sessions.

It is a good idea to present the parents/carers with a laminated version of the prayer for parents, or some other suitable prayer. This is also at the back of the Activity book. You may need to be aware of the variety of languages and backgrounds within the parish community and the need to provide the necessary help.

In most situations the programme will be part of parish life and the leaders/catechists will be people willing to make a commitment to this ministry. In some areas, particularly the more remote rural areas, it may be that groups of parents will come together and deliver the programme, or that parents may use it with their children.

What is in the programme?

The programme is set firmly within the context of the Catholic faith and is concerned to offer the opportunity for children to develop a personal relationship with God: the Father who creates, the Son who redeems and the Holy Spirit who makes us holy – and the opportunity to come to know and love their faith as they journey through life as friends of Jesus.

The children are offered a systematic presentation of the Incarnation, Passion, Death and Resurrection of Jesus Christ, which is the Paschal Mystery, the supreme event that unites Christians in faith. They are invited to learn and understand the Christian message and way of life, appropriate to the age and stage of their development. [10]

Children who are not baptised

The experience in a number of parishes is that more and more children over the age of eight are coming forward for baptism and therefore are in need of appropriate initiation into the Faith. In order to respond to that need, the new programme includes a separate book on the CICCA (Christian Initiation of Children of Catechetical Age) as well as some cross-referencing to it in the main programme. The norms for CICCA are outlined in Part II, Chapter 1 of the Rite of Christian Initiation of Adults (RCIA #252-330). The rite states:

"This form of the rite of Christian initiation is intended for children not baptized as infants, who have attained the use of reason and are of catechetical age. They seek Christian initiation either at the direction of their parents or guardians or, with parental permission, on their own initiative. Such children are capable of receiving and nurturing a personal faith and of recognising an obligation of conscience." [11]

How does the programme work?

It offers a range of sessions for different age groups, abilities and experiences. A variety of prayer and celebration experiences, formal and informal, is suggested, to enable the children to reflect upon and develop their own prayer life.

The programme includes teaching about the sacraments. Since the local parish will have its own programme of preparation for the children's first reception of sacraments, explicit preparation is not part of *I Call You Friends*. In Book 1 the sessions about the sacraments of the Eucharist and Reconciliation will a good foundation for and complement their sacramental preparation. The children's understanding will continue to deepen with Book 2, the post Communion sessions.

The programme includes teaching about the liturgical year but it is not a resource to support The Liturgy of the Word with Children, which takes place during the Sunday celebration of the Eucharist.

---

7 Rite of Baptism for Children 1969, Committee on English in the Liturgy, Inc. All Rights Reserved ICEL.
8 CC 2207.
9 cf Gaudium et Spes (1965) 52:1.
10 cf CCC, 24.
11 Christian Initiation, General Introduction, 1988, Congregation for Divine Worship and the Discipline of the Sacraments. RCIA #242.

The foundation of *I Call You Friends*

There are some basic questions about life[12] which are common to all humankind namely:

- ❖ *Where do I come from?*
- ❖ *Who am I?*
- ❖ *Why am I here?*

These questions concern the mystery of life, its dignity and purpose. They are part of every person's search for meaning. For the Christian the search for meaning in life finds its response in the mystery of God, Father, Son and Holy Spirit, revealed in the life of Jesus Christ. In *I Call you Friends* this search is explored in Scripture and Tradition.

The *Catechism of the Catholic Church* drew its strength and inspiration from the documents of the Second Vatican Council (1962-1965). *I Call You Friends* is underpinned by and draws its vision from these documents.[13]

GOD SPEAKS – finding meaning in life

At the heart of the programme is the Dogmatic Constitution on Divine Revelation (*Dei Verbum*, 1965).

God Speaks: which breathes life into part one of *The Catechism of the Catholic Church: The Profession of Faith*. When we believe we respond to God with faith. God reveals himself to all human persons. God enlightens each human person with abundant grace, as minds and hearts search for meaning in life.[14]

THE CHURCH – Community of Faith

The Dogmatic Constitution on the Church (*Lumen Gentium*, 1964).

Light to the Nations: is further expanded in *The Catechism of the Catholic Church, The Profession of Faith*, and refers to the gathering of God's people. The Church can mean the worshipping community, but it also extends to whole community of believers, local and universal. The Church draws her life from the Word, (Scripture) and the Body of Christ (the Eucharist) and so becomes what she is already is: Christ's body.[15]

CHRISTIAN LIVING: Joy and hope – Way of life

The Pastoral Constitution on the Church in the World of Today (*Gaudium et Spes*, 1964).

Joy and Hope: links into part three of *The Catechism of the Catholic Church, Life in Christ*. The dignity of the human person is found in the Christian belief that each human person is created in the image and likeness of God.[16] This life in God through Jesus Christ is celebrated and supported throughout the liturgical year, which follows the journey of Jesus' earthly life.

LITURGY: Celebration – Celebration in symbol and ritual

The Constitution on the Sacred Liturgy (*Sacrosanctum Concilium*, 1963).

Celebration: is further elaborated in parts two and four of *The Catechism of the Catholic Church, the Celebration of the Christian Mystery* and in the section on Prayer. In the liturgy, especially in the Eucharist, the work of our redemption is completed. It is through the liturgy we are able to express in our lives the mystery of Christ.[17]

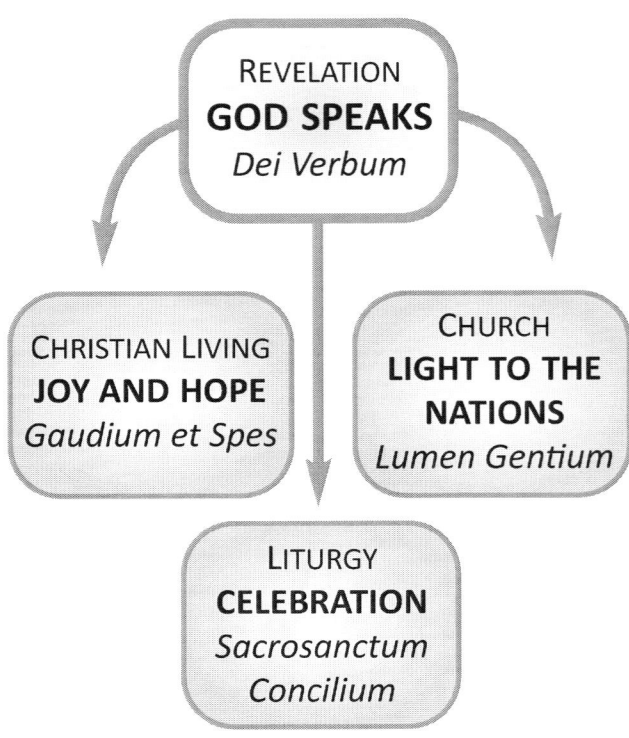

---

12 CCC (1994) 282
13 The references from Catechism of the Catholic Church are given exactly as they appear in the text, which is not in inclusive language,
14 cf. CCC 26
15 cf 751, 752
16 cf CCC1700
17 cf. *Sacrosanctum Concilium* (1963)

Introduction – The Themes

THE THEMES

Three themes are developed with increasing depth throughout the programme: Church, Sacraments and Christian Living. *I Call You Friends* would normally begin in September, but if this is not possible some adjustment will need to be made.

1 The Church

The Church themes occur in every season and each theme gradually builds on the understanding of the previous one.
Each theme is developed in three sessions.

Autumn: My Story
| My family | Domestic Church

To start the year, *I Call You Friends* begins with My Story: the family. The Church honours the family with the title Domestic Church because it is there that parents *'by their word and example are the first heralds of faith with regard to their children.'* [18]

Spring: Our Story
| Local Community | Local Church

After Christmas, the children explore the theme of local Church which is *Our* Story. The parish is where people gather together to celebrate and show care and love for each other.[19] The diocese is the community of the Christian faithful, gathered in union with its bishop.[20]

Summer: The Story
| The worldwide community
| Universal Church

The year finishes with The Story of the worldwide community: the universal Church. *'The Church is the people God gathered in the whole world.'* [21] *'The order and harmony of the created world results from the diversity of beings and from the relationships that exist among them'* [22]

2 Sacraments

Sacramental themes occur in every season and each one gradually builds on the understanding of the previous theme. Each theme is developed in three sessions.

Autumn: Belonging
| Born into Christ's life
| Baptism *(Book 2 Confirmation – Marriage – Ordination)*

Following on from the family – Domestic Church, the theme of Baptism introduces the understanding of initiation into the Catholic Church. *'The faithful are born anew by Baptism, strengthened by the Sacrament of Confirmation, and receive in the Eucharist the food of eternal life.'* [23] In Book 2 the children learn about the Sacraments of Confirmation, Ordination and Marriage. The Sacraments of Ordination and Marriage are directed towards the salvation of others and help to support the People of God on their pilgrim journey through life.[24]

Spring: Relating
| God's love in our lives | Eucharist

After learning about the local Church community, the Sacrament of the Eucharist is explored. This is the sacrament of communion with Christ and the Church. It is at the heart of *I Call You Friends*.

Summer: Inter-relating
| Service to the community
| Reconciliation *(Book 2 Sacrament of the Sick).*

The sessions on the Sacrament of Reconciliation reflect God's love and mercy and the joy and challenge of relationships, which are celebrated in this sacrament. The post-communion children will learn about the Sacrament of the Anointing of the Sick, which strengthens, forgives and unites the person more closely to Christ. These are sacraments of healing. ▷

---

18 Lumen Gentium 11 and cf CCC1656
19 cf CCC 2179
20 cf CCC 833
21 CCC 752
22 CCC 341

23 Cf CCC 121224
24 CCC 1534

THE THEMES continued

3 Christian Living

The Christian living themes occur in every season and each theme gradually builds on the understanding of the previous theme. Each theme is developed in three sessions.

Autumn: Loving
| Celebrating life
| Advent/Christmas

The Advent/Christmas theme considers the gift of God's love in Jesus. It celebrates the wonderful gift of Jesus and offers the witness of loving as a way of life. *'The Word became flesh so that we might know God's love.'*[25]

Spring: Giving
| The cost of life | Lent, Easter

In the Spring Lent and Easter are explored. Jesus' love for humankind knows no boundary. Jesus offered his life and gave an example of self-giving as a way of life. *'Easter is not simply one feast among others, but the feast of feasts.'*[26] *'The Resurrection... remains at the very heart of the mystery of faith as something which transcends and surpasses history.'*[27]

Summer: Serving in love
| Feasts to celebrate
| Pentecost

The sessions on Ascension and the celebration of Pentecost complete the Easter story and show how the gift of the Holy Spirit strengthens the community, enabling Christians to give witness to a life of joyful service. *'In this age of the Church, Christ now lives and acts in and with his Church, in a new way appropriate to this new age.'*[28]

* * *

Besides these times there are also particular themes, prayers and hymns associated with certain months of the year; e.g.

- May: the month of Our Lady
- June: the Sacred Heart
- October: Rosary
- November: prayers for the dead

It would be helpful to mention these themes, prayers and hymns in the months in which they occur. The prayers can be adapted for the children from a simple prayer book or the Internet.

25 CCC 458
26 CCC 1169
27 CCC 647
28 CCC 1076

The Word of God: Scripture and Tradition

God is revealed to us through Scripture[29] and Tradition.[30] Scripture is the heart of the Tradition, which is what has been handed down to us. It continues in the Church tradition as a living and developing reality.

The first section of the Bible, which we know as the Old Testament, is drwan from the Hebrew Scriptures. These texts were of such importance to the Jewish people that they have ben carefully preserved and acknowledged to be Holy Scripture. Similarly, the Christian people from the earliest times preserved their own writings concerning Jesus of Nazareth and their faith in him. These are the foundational writings of the Church, known to us as the New Testament.

In the Scriptures God speaks. We acknowledge them to be the Word of God to us. The written word of Scripture proclaims the love of God for all the peoples of the world. The message of the inspired word is summed up in Jesus, the Son of God, who is the fullness of God's revelation to us. He is the one who frees us from sin and death, and leads us to life.

The writers of the Scriptures used a variety of ways to communicate God's message. They used stories, statements, songs and letters. They showed how God was present in the life of the people. Story telling was a particular feature of daily life in Palestine. Jesus would have come to know the stories of what God had done for Israel. When he told his own stories he rooted them in the everyday experiences of

29 The children's resource GOD'S STORY contains most of the scripture used in the programme.
30 The children's resource CHURCH'S STORY contains most of the tradition used in the programme.

his listeners. They tell of ploughing, fishing, sowing seeds, baking, losing and finding.

In the Scriptures God speaks to us in human words, in accessible forms. Tradition is the continuing living transmission of God's word. We see it in the way the good news taught by Jesus is passed on by his disciples and throughout the history of the Church.

Tradition grows and develops, as more and more disciples understand the good news, and as new circumstances require new insights. Scripture and Tradition, which are guided by the Spirit, are living realities. This understanding frees us from a fundamentalist viewpoint which sees Scripture as static. Scripture and Tradition enlighten and transform our lives in a changing world. The Gospel of Matthew reminds us that we are called to be like the householder *'...who brings out of his storeroom things both new and old'* (Matthew 13:52).

Miracles and Parables

A miracle may be understood as an event which is contrary to nature. However, St Augustine in his *City of God*[31] suggested that it is an event which is contrary to what we know of nature, as our understanding of nature is limited. Many events in the Old Testament were considered miraculous, the most notable being the Exodus from Egypt and the parting of Sea of Reeds.[32] All miraculous events were regarded by the Jewish people as signs of the power of God and are part of God's liberating activity. They brought to people's attention God's love in action.

Miracle Stories in the New Testament

The first words on the lips of Jesus in Mark's Gospel are "The time is fulfilled – the Kingdom of God is at hand." Miracle stories in the New Testament are before all else signs that the Kingdom of God is at hand. In his ministry Jesus welcomed all who were excluded from the community for whatever reason. The miracle stories invariably restore these people to community – no wonder the word 'amazement' regularly reflects the reaction of the crowd to Jesus in these expressions of his healing ministry. Miracle Stories are a call to a way of life that transforms. They invite us to see the world through the eyes of Jesus – eyes of inclusion, welcome and healing.

Appropriate/relevant miracles stories are introduced, when children have the ability to understand them more accurately.

The Parables of Jesus

While parables are a significant part of the preaching of Jesus, he did not invent the form. One of the most famous parables in the Old Testament is the story told by the prophet Nathan to King David after the murder of Uriah the Hittite the husband of Bathsheba (2 Samuel 12:1-7). The rich man takes the poor man's lamb to feed his guest. The story provokes David's anger against this rich man's injustice. Then Nathan says to David *"You are the man."*

Jesus' parables are challenging. The temptation to tell a *'nice story'* may lead us to reduce his teaching to bland moralising. Jesus' parables challenge us personally. Parables, like miracles, are signs that the Kingdom of God is at hand. Parable tellers put their lives on the line because they invite their hearers to a new way of seeing and acting in the world.

---

31 cf City of God XXI: 5
32 Exodus 14

Prayer and Celebration

Prayer is the language of love; it is listening to and being present to God. It sustains our living relationship with God. As a community, we pray in different ways, formal and informal prayer, as well as private personal prayer. Sometimes we pray together using well-known prayers that are treasured by the family of the Church. Sometimes we simply talk to God in our own words and sometimes we are still and we listen.

Prayer and Celebration with Children

Here are some suggestions to help children to grow in their relationship with the mystery we call God.

FOR PARENTS

The start of the day

Find an opportunity to pray together, beginning with the Sign of the Cross slowly and thoughtfully and then say:

> 'We thank you for this new day.
> Bless us all we pray
> Be with us as we work and play
> and help us love you more and more.
>   Amen'

or some other simple words you and your child have made up together, to offer the day to God.

Bedtime

This is an opportunity to be together with your child, to share what is happening in their life, to be aware of the Mystery of God's presence with them and to develop a healthy habit of prayer for life: daily reflection and awareness of God's love always surrounding them. Encourage your child to choose a religious picture or statue, holy water etc. that they would like to keep near them where they sleep. (There may be a 'holy shop' in your parish). They could use this a a prayer focus. Try to create a sense of peace and comfort.

Thinking things over at the end of the day

✶ Perhaps light a candle or a night-light and look at the flame together quietly.
✶ Talk about the day with your child.
✶ You might like to say something about what made you happy and what was good for you and then thank God together.
✶ Talk together about anything that made you or your child sad during the day?
✶ Is there anything you are sorry about thhat you would like to share?
✶ You both ask for God's help and forgiveness to make things better. Here is a prayer that wisely focuses on God's love:

> God, Our Father,
> thank you for loving me.
> I am sorry for the times
>   I have not been loving.
> Help me always to live like Jesus.
>   Amen.

✶ Ask your child "Who do you want to pray for?" "Let's ask God to bless them."
✶ Say a short night prayer together. There is one in the children's activity book; end with the Sign of the Cross. You may like to make this sign on the child's forehead and say words such as:

> "May God bless you and keep you safe tonight". (You could use the holy water.)

✶ *Home is a Holy Place*, see the website, is an initiative of the Bishops' Conference and is worth looking at for further resources for developing the faith at home.

Meal times

Sharing food together is sharing life and love! Try to give the children this experience and begin with asking for a blessing on the meal, thanking God for the gift of food etc. Let the children take a turn in praying the blessing.

In church

Help your children to feel at home in church. They can bless themselves making the Sign of the Cross with holy water as they go into church to remind them of their Baptism. You can help them to 'genuflect', that is to bend down on their right knee before the Blessed Sacrament reserved in the tabernacle. Children love gestures, they pray with their bodies, so when everyone prays the Our Father let them hold out their hands or hold hands etc. Give the children a simple Mass book so they can follow what is happening and match the pictures or read the text. After Mass they enjoy lighting candles, a sign of our continuing prayer.

Resources

There are excellent books, DVDs etc which convey gospel values e.g. *'The Nativity Story,' 'Miracle Maker'* or *'The Prince of Egypt'* DVDs, gospel stories on DVD, IMFH multimedia, books such as: *'Guess how much I love you'* [33] and the *'Friends of Jesus,'* [34] series which you can use to read or watch together and talk about. This can also be a way of praying. The memory of your closeness and time spent together will always be precious and is a living sign to them of God's loving closeness and gentle care. The stories touch on important realities such as a child's discovery of him/herself.

FOR PARENTS AND CATECHISTS

There are many prayer books available. Use whatever seems suitable.

Litany prayers: the parent/catechist says a simple statement or request and the children answer with the response that stays the same throughout. You can be very inventive but here are some examples:

> For our family and friends:
> **We thank you, Lord**
> For another new day:
> **We thank you, Lord**
> For our toys and our books:
> **We thank you, Lord**
> For work and for play:
> **We thank you, Lord**
> For children in hospital:
> **Take Care of them, Lord**
> For those without homes:
> **Take Care of them, Lord**
> For people who are lonely:
> **Take Care of them, Lord**
> For people who are hungry:
> **Take Care of them, Lord**

Gestures: Praying with our bodies, with our whole selves, is so important. It is good to encourage children to do this as they are not self-conscious – it just comes naturally! Some catechists may be able to show the children sign language gestures to use to accompany words such as *Jesus, love, sorry* etc. Children will happily make up their own gestures to show praise, thanksgiving, and asking. Sometimes we stand up to pray; sometimes we kneel; sometimes we sit; sometimes we dance; sometimes we hold hands. Try to be creative and sensitive to what is best in a given situation.

Formal prayers

The following grid offers some ideas and guideline about the prayers children may know or be familiar with at different stages. Some children have more difficulty than others in learning prayers off by heart, so frequent use of the prayers at home or in the sessions is helpful. It is less important that the children are word prefect than that they understand and enjoy praying.

There is a downloadable pack of prayers in symbol supported text available from the Widgit website.

Know	Be familiar with
The Sign of the Cross	Some phrases from the Psalms
Our Father	Prayer to the Holy Spirit
Hail Mary	Short scriptural quotes
Glory be	The Rosary
Morning prayer	The Stations of the Cross
Night prayer	The Creed
A prayer of sorrow 'sorry prayer'	The Gloria
Grace before meals	
Prayer for the faithful departed	
Lamb of God	
Mass responses	
Holy, holy	

---

33 Published by Walker Books 1994 ISBN 0 7445 3224 8.
34 Victoria Hummell r.a., McCrimmon Publishing Co. Ltd.

Preparing for for the children's sessions

Each book provides a process for the delivery of every session. This may be adapted to the needs of the group. Essential resources to accompany each book are copies of GOD'S STORY[35] 1, 2 or 3, which contain most of the scripture used throughout the programme. Copies of CHURCH'S STORY[36] 1, 2 or 3 are also essential as they contain pictures and text which support the delivery of the sessions on sacrament and church. There is a CD-ROM for both books providing clip art and text which can be used as a print out or on a PowerPoint if one is available.

The 'IMFH Friends' multi-media CD-ROM has been designed by IMFH Publications[37] to accompany Book 1 but may also be useful with older children who have special needs.

CAFOD: check when the Family Fast Days occur (Autumn and Spring) and use some of their material in your sessions, and talk about ideas for raising funds for CAFOD projects. Contact your local CAFOD representative, and check the section for primary schools on the CAFOD website www.cafod.org.uk

Leaders' preparation

To help you prepare well for the sessions:

* Check the last session to ensure continuity.
* Read through the details of the session, especially the activities you may want to adapt to suit your group of children.
* Check the pages in GOD'S STORY or CHURCH'S STORY and read the relevant adult's notes at the end of each book.
* Check you have all the resources you need.
* Check the room you are going to use to ensure it is a safe and a welcoming environment.

Team preparation

If you are working in a team you may want to do all of the above together as a group and perhaps share your own understanding of the theme you are presenting. You might use the introduction on the IMFH CD to do this.

The setting

Wherever the sessions take place, it is important to ensure that it is a special place, a sacred place. Attention needs to be given to the prayer focus in the room. It is best kept simple – a cloth in the current liturgical colour, a candle, a copy of the scriptures, or children's Bible and a symbol relevant to the season, for example an Advent wreath, an Easter garden, a crib, statue or picture of Our Lady, a rosary, a tray of sand for Lent, a crucifix; a Baptism robe; etc. It is a good idea to get the children to help with the setting and to take turns in lighting or putting out the candle if they are old enough (see the Health and Safety guide at the end of this book).

Liturgical colours for the drapes to be used

* GREEN for the ordinary times of the year
* PURPLE for Advent and Lent signifying penance
* RED for Pentecost and for feasts of martyrs
* WHITE or GOLD for important feasts like Christmas and Easter and for saints who are not martyrs
* BLUE is associated with Mary

The use of music

Music can be used to enhance the sessions: for example, to set a mood, to facilitate prayer, and to draw out certain themes or emphasise key points. The four CD music set that accompanies this book may be of use for this (see page 82). There is something very special and immediate about having live music if there are musicians available. Where this is not possible, play the CD with the children supplementing the music with singing and the playing of instruments.

It may seem obvious, but choose music appropriate to the theme; for example, for the liturgical season, or the subject you are addressing. Don't feel that music always has to be used. There are times when just the human voice reading or silence carries the moment more meaningfully.

The songs given in the text are suggestions, there may be songs which are appropriate and are used in the parish which the children are more familiar with.

A key to the music references, used within the text, can be found on the resources page at the back of the book.

---

35 National Project, Rejoice Publications 2002
36 National Project, Rejoice Publications 2006
37 IMFH Publications, 1 South Hill, Upton Grey, Hampshire RG25 2SH. www.imfhpublications.com

THE SESSIONS

Within each group there may be a variety of experiences and understanding, especially if a child has not consistently attended all the sessions. Parents and catechists may find it helpful to be flexible in deciding which book is appropriate for an individual child. In parishes where there are large numbers of children, it may be helpful to have sub groups with a variety of levels of activities. There are suggestions and ideas for resources for use with children who have special needs. These ideas could be used with any group.

If you have a group of children who are using Book 1 or Book 2 for a second year, try to vary and develop the activities and perhaps instead of using the ACTIVITY BOOK for a second year use a scrapbook instead which would allow the children to develop further thoughts and ideas.

Each session follows the same pattern:

Before you begin   A

In preparation for each session there is a text of Scripture and a quote from the Catechism of the Catholic Church for the leaders to reflect upon at their own level. You may wish to read beyond the quotes offered.

This is what you are trying to communicate   B

This outlines the overall focus of the session. It would be good to follow the guidance given in the programme about the content as it is intended to be systematic. However, you may wish to adapt the way it is delivered according to the age and experience of the group. If, occasionally, an important topical issue arises, make use of it.

There are three sessions for each theme.

Each session will last from between 30 minutes to an hour depending on age and circumstances. The focus of each session builds on the previous one.

How we might go about it   C

There are five basic components for each session,

1. Welcome and gathering
2. Let's remember
3. Let's share
4. Let's discover
5. Reflect and connect

Occasionally there are suggestions for follow-up with parents.

Special needs   D

The material in this programme is intended for use with children of different abilities including children who may have a learning difficulty or disability. If you do have any children with particular needs in your group it is important that you talk to the parents/carers to find out how best to enable these children to enjoy and benefit from the sessions. You will need to find out what about the physical access which is needed. It may probably be a good idea to invite the parents/carers to stay in the sessions, at least until their children are confident in the group.

Consideration needs to be given to how you can integrate all the children so they help one another. All children benefit from different ways of learning and when consideration is given to providing approaches and resources to include those with special needs, then a more enriching faith and learning experience for all is achieved.

When working with all children there are three key aspects to teaching and learning:

1. Gaining and sustaining attention
2. Providing enjoyable and accessible learning experiences
3. Sharing The Good News

The following are tried and tested approaches which take into account a wide range of special needs:

* Providing opportunities to eat or taste, to look at, to smell, to touch, to listen to and to and engage with (a multisensory approach).[38]

* Providing a variety of materials, toys, food, interactive objects which engage children's curiosity and involve them in sharing and taking turns (motivational stimuli).

* Music – songs to sing, music to move to and especially songs with sign language and action songs. Music is often an effective way of marking the start and finish of a session and creating a sense of celebration or reflection/stillness.

* Sign language and text accompanied by symbols or illustrations are essential tools to support understanding of the spoken and written word.[39] ▷

---

[38] This will provide experiences for children with sensory impairments, Autism Spectrum Disorders, Profound and multiple learning disabilities and communication disorders.

[39] Different systems in use include British Sign Language, Makaton, Singalong. Widgit software.

16 | Introduction – The Sessions

THE SESSIONS continued

* Using a variety of media to animate a story and bring a theme to life, for example, objects named in the story or key to the theme, the use of puppets or role play.

* Reassurance and predictability are especially important. A familiar structure for each session builds confidence and if a change is planned it is important to let children know. Some children may benefit from a visual schedule to guide them through the sequence of activities.

* An accessible learning environment with facilities for wheelchair users and one in which, when possible, there are no distractions.

> This sign indicates activities suitable for children with special needs. The following website www.widgit.com/resources/, will have some symbol supported text which could be used for such things as lotto games, where the children match the pictures and talk about them. These symbols may be a useful and fun way of learning for children of all abilities.
>
> See the Resources section for more ideas.

LEADING THE SESSIONS

1 Welcome and gathering E

It is good to have a word of welcome for the children and their parents, maybe someone at the door to welcome everyone by name as they come in. New children will need a special welcome and introduction.

Once everyone is settled, have a short moment of stillness, maybe ring a bell or have some quiet music. It is good to have a familiar ritual each week. When everyone is still, make the Sign of the Cross and have a short prayer. For simple naming, greeting or gathering songs see 'Connecting with RE' and 'Causeway Prospects'.

2 Let's remember F

Briefly recall the last session. It may be appropriate to remember what the children were asked to do at home with their parents. They might like to share something from the activity book.

3 Let's share G

The children are encouraged either to share their personal experience, listen to a story, look at  a picture or listen to a piece of music which will enable them to examine and reflect on an aspect of life experience which will raise questions. This section includes some key questions, for which there are no right or wrong answers, but will help the children to think and so engage with their own understanding. If children choose not to share, that is alright. Sometimes it may help if the catechist gives an example from their own life.

4 Let's discover H

This is the heart of every session. Here the children are introduced to the Christian understanding of the mystery of God and human life as expressed in the life of Jesus Christ. This is done by learning about Scripture, the Tradition and teaching of the Church, prayer, psalms, hymns and the lives of outstanding Christians. This part of the process may be delivered in a variety of creative and practical ways through drama, art, song, dance, poetry.

The suggested activities are indicated by a separate heading. For some sessions two levels of activities are offered: **A** for the younger or less experienced child and **B** for the older or more experienced child, possibly the children who are in the second year of the programme. Some older and more able children may be able to use the Bible[40] themselves to look up references or find further scripture.

5 Reflect and connect I

As the children gather around the prayer focus once more the sessions are concluded by recalling what has been learnt. There is a short period of reflection with the Scripture, prayer and song which may have been used in the session.

The Activity book J

Children will have their own activity book, for use in the session or at home. It may be helpful to read through the relevant page in the activity book with the children to ensure that they have understood it. These are not homework books

---
40 Good News Bibles are to be recommended for this age group.

and if the child does not complete the page, it might be finished during the session. The activity book ought to be enjoyable for the child not onerous. It is hoped that parents/carers may help and work with their children at home so reinforcing what has been experienced in the sessions.

With parents K

It is important to think about the role of parents, and where possible include links with the home. Some sessions have specific suggestions for activities at home. The Activity book will make these links.

Perhaps some parents may be willing to help with the sessions. In rural areas and for a variety of reasons, parents themselves may need to use the programme at home with their own children.

Other resources L

This contains suggestions for further resources that might be helpful. Please note that although website addresses might be given in the text there is no guarantee of the accuracy and is is probably best to do a search yourself.

Don't forget M

Offers a few points that might be worth considering.

Attendance: Try to include children who attend irregularly and help them to join in as well as possible.

Debriefing of leaders: it would be helpful for the leaders to spend a few moments after the session reflecting on what has gone well and what they might need for the next session. It might be helpful to end this time together with a prayer.

A General Overview of books 1 and 2

THEMES	PRE-COMMUNION SESSIONS 1	PRE-COMMUNION SESSIONS 2	PRE-COMMUNION SESSIONS 3	POST-COMMUNION SESSIONS 1	POST-COMMUNION SESSIONS 2	POST-COMMUNION SESSIONS 3
Domestic church My Story – Family	**Myself** God[41] knows and loves me	**Beginnings** God is at every beginning	**Home & Families** God gave me my family. God as parent	**Qualities** Created in the image and likeness of God	**People: God's joy** God's dream for every family	**Families** God who never stops loving
Baptism Confirmation Belonging – Born into Christ's life	**Welcome** Baptism; a welcome to the family	**Together** Church family gathers for a baby's baptism	**Signs & Symbols** Signs and symbols in baptism	**Promises** Promises made at baptism	**Initiation** Confirmation: a time to renew baptismal promises	**Life choices** Christian life Marriage / ordination
Advent / Christmas Loving – Celebrating life	**Preparing** Preparing with Mary	**Visitors** The coming of Jesus	**Gift** God's gift of love & friendship in Jesus	**Birthdays** Looking forward to Jesus' birthday	**Hope** Waiting in joyful hope for Jesus; the promised one	**Expectation** Jesus was born to show God to the world
Local church Our Story – Local Community	**Journeys** Christian families journey with Jesus	**People who do special jobs** People in the parish family	**Celebrate** People celebrate in church	**Books** The books used in Church	**My parish** Life in the local Christian community: the parish	**My diocese** Continuing Jesus' mission in the diocese
Eucharist Relating – God's love in our lives	**Gathering** The parish family gather to celebrate the Eucharist	**Meals** Mass; Jesus' special meal	**Thank you** Mass: a special way to say thank you to God for Jesus	**Thanksgiving** Thanksgiving for Jesus	**Memories** The Eucharist: the living memorial of Jesus	**Unity** Eucharist enables people to live in communion
Lent / Easter Giving – The cost of life	**Growing** Lent: getting ready for Easter	**Change** Lent: a time to change	**New life** Preparing to celebrate Jesus' new life at Easter	**Giving all** Lent: a time to remember Jesus' total giving	**Self discipline** Celebrating growth into new life	**Death & new life** Celebrating Jesus' death and Resurrection
Pentecost Serving in love – Feasts to celebrate	**Good News** The Good New of Jesus	**Holiday & holydays** Pentecost: the feast of the Holy Spirit	**Messengers** Passing on the Good News of Jesus	**Energy** Gifts of the Holy Spirit	**Transformation** celebration of the Spirit's transforming power	**Witness** The Holy Spirit enables people to become witnesses
Reconciliation Inter-relating service to the community	**Friends** Friends of Jesus	**Rules** Rules of the Christian family	**Being sorry** Asking for forgiveness	**Choices** The importance of the examination of conscience	**Building bridges** Admitting wrong, being reconciled with others and God	**Healing** The Sacrament of the Sick
Universal Church The story born into the worldwide community	**All around us** God's wonderful world	**My place** A place for prayer	**Treasure** God's love for everyone	**Neighbours** Neighbours share God's world	**Difference** Different saints show people what God is like	**Outreach** Work of the worldwide Christian family

---

41 The word God is used here to refer God the Creator, Father Almighty.

Introduction – A General Overview | 19

OVERVIEW OF BOOK 2 SESSIONS

THEMES			
Domestic church My Story – Family	1. Qualities Created in the image and likeness of God	2. People: God's joy God's dream for every family	3. Families God who never stops loving
Baptism Confirmation Belonging – Born into Christ's life	4. Called Baptism, a new life	5. Confirm Confirmation: a sacrament to strengthen the baptised person's relationship with God and the Church	6. Life choices Christian life Marriage / Ordination
Advent / Christmas Loving – Celebrating life	7. Birthdays Looking forward to Jesus' birthday	8. Hope Waiting in joyful hope for Jesus; the promised one	9. Expectation Jesus was born to show God to the world
Local church Our Story – Local Community	10. Books The books used in church	11. My parish Life in the local Christian community: the parish	12. My diocese Continuing Jesus' mission in the diocese
Eucharist Relating – God's love in our lives	13. Thanksgiving Thanksgiving for Jesus	14. Memories The Eucharist – the living memorial of Jesus	15. Unity The Eucharist enables people to live in communion
Lent / Easter Giving – The cost of life	16. Giving all Lent, a time to remember Jesus' total giving	17. Self-discipline Celebrating growth into new life	18. Death & new life Celebrating Jesus' death & Resurrection
Pentecost Serving in love – Feasts to celebrate	19. Energy Gifts of the Holy Spirit	20. Transformation Celebration of the Spirit's transforming power	21. Witness The Holy Spirit enables people to become witnesses
Reconciliation Inter-relating service to the community	22. Choices The importance of examination of conscience	23. Building bridges Admitting wrong, being reconciled with othersw and God	24. Healing The Sacrament of the Sick
Universal Church The story born into the worldwide community	25. Neighbours Neighbours share God's world	26. Difference Different saints show people what God is like.	27. Outreach Work of the worldwide Christian family

Autumn Theme 1

MY STORY | FAMILY | DOMESTIC CHURCH

Domestic Church: We, who are the People of God, make up the Community of Faith. My Story is that I was born into life. This theme is about considering people who love and care for us and remembering that God knows and loves everyone from the very beginning of their lives.

SESSION 1:
Qualities

Created in the image and likeness of God

Before you begin

Reflect on what this means to you:

> 'God created human beings making them to be like himself. He created them male and female.'
> Genesis 1:27

From the Catechism of the Catholic Church, 355; 356:

'Man occupies a unique place in creation: he is in "the image of God"; in his own nature he unites the spiritual and material worlds; he is created "male and female"; God established him in his friendship... he alone is called to share, by knowledge and love, in God's own life. It was for this end that he was created and this is the fundamental reason for his dignity.'

This is what you are trying to communicate

God made us like Himself to share in His own life. The dignity of all human beings stems directly from this. Each person is gifted by God; they have to develop these qualities through knowledge and love for themselves.

| 22 | Autumn Theme 1 | Session 1 | Leader's Book 2

You will need
- *PRAYER FOCUS* with: candle, cloth
- Newspaper cuttings of local/national heroes.
- Copy the qualities from Isaiah from God's Story 3, p.63 on cards.
- God's Story 3, p.147.
- A microphone or something which could be used as an imitation microphone.

How we might go about it

Welcome and gathering

Have a short moment of silence. While the candle is lit, make the Sign of the Cross.

Have a gathering prayer about God's gifts to us.

Read '*Remember God always*' from God's Story 3, p.55 (Based on Ecclesiastes 11:8-10).

After the reading sing: '*Rejoice in the Lord always*', (CFE 617).

Let's share

Talk about what the word 'qualities' means. (This topic uses the word 'qualities' to mean e.g. kindness, love, care, courage, generosity, the gifts of the Beatitudes. 'Talents' usually refer to gifts like the ability to play a musical instrument or to excel in a sport.)

Give some examples of personal qualities that can be seen in others whom we admire e.g. Bring in newspapers cuttings or a display of pictures of some local/national courageous person.

Encourage the children to give their own examples e.g. "*I like…….. because she/he ………*" (name the personal quality). Explain that we all have qualities.

Some key questions to wonder about

* Which qualities do you most admire about the people we have talked about and why?
* How do you think these qualities were developed?
* What personal qualities do you think you have?
* What personal qualities would you like to have and why?

Let's discover

A. Read Isaiah 58:3-8 from God's Story 3, p.63 (you may need to read this twice). Ask the children to listen out for the qualities they especially like. These are the qualities which show us something of God. Invite the children to choose a card with a quality on it.

Some key questions to wonder about

* What does this quality mean for you and why did you choose it?
* Do you know anyone who has this quality?
* How do they show it?

Activity

❖ The leader also takes a card and says why they have taken that quality and tells a short story to model the activity. In pairs the children make up a short story about the qualities they have chosen and act it out or tell the story together.

B. Read together, '*You are a holy people*' from God's Story 3, p.147, (based on Colossians 3:12-17). (You could just use the first paragraph). Think and talk about this together. Remember that all our qualities are gifts from God for us to use to show love and care.

Some questions to wonder about

✸ Which quality listed in this reading did you like best and why?

✸ Do you know someone who has this quality?

✸ How do they show it?

Activity

❖ In pairs invite the children to make up a short story about one of the qualities.

 Play 'Being like Jesus' lotto game; match 'qualities' symbols to 'people I love' symbols.

Activity book

Talk about the page in the Activity book.

Reflect and connect

A prayerful moment, thanking God for their own qualities: Using the stories as a 'good news' TV bulletin, the children report back from the scene of where the qualities have been shown.

The children can end their bulletin by saying *'and it's back to you in the Good News studio'*.

End by singing: *'Make me a channel of your peace'*, (ICYF-CD2 / AYOC147).

SESSION 2:
People
God's Joy – God's dream for every family

Before you begin

Reflect on what this means to you:

> 'I drew them to me with affection and love. I picked them up and held them to my cheek; I bent down to them and fed them.'
>
> Hosea 11:4

From the Catechism of the Catholic Church, 357:

Being in the image of God the human individual possesses the dignity of a 'person', who is not just something but someone.

You will need

- ❋ PRAYER FOCUS with: candle, cloth
- ❋ Music e.g. 'I hope you dance'
- ❋ God's Story 3, p.67 'God sings for joy!'
- ❋ Some hymn books,
- ❋ If possible a few percussion instruments.
- ❋ For children using this for a second year some blank postcards.

This is what you are trying to communicate

The God who has created us loves and cares for us. God takes delight in us. Because of that, we have dignity.

How we might go about it

Welcome and gathering

Have a short quiet moment. Whilst the candle is being lit, make the Sign of the Cross. Then listen to some cheerful music e.g. 'I hope you dance.'

Read the following scripture from Zephaniah 3:17, (God's Story 3, p.67).

> 'The Lord your God is with you.
> The Lord will take delight in you.
> And in his love he will give you new life.
> He will sing and be joyful over you.'

Let's remember

Ask the children to remember the last session, share/discuss the page in the Activity book from the previous session. They may recall:

- ❋ Their own qualities and how they share them with others.
- ❋ What qualities tell us more about God?

Let's share

Think about the people you know. Who is the person who makes you happy? Who do you go to when you are upset? Who makes you feel loved? (The children may want to reflect on this quietly in their hearts. Be aware that this may stir some deep emotion so ensure that this time is treated sensitively.)

Some questions to wonder about

* What is special about that person?
* How do they make you feel loved?
* Who are you special for?

Let's discover

A. The birth of Samuel from God's Story 3, p.33. This is a story from the Old Testament, that part of the Bible which tells God's Story before the coming of Jesus. Tell the story of Hannah. Explain about Hannah longing for a baby and her joy when she gives birth to Samuel her son. Read through the text of Hannah's prayer together. (It is in the children's Activity book.)

Some questions to wonder about

* Which part of Hannah's prayer do you like best and why?
* Think of a time when God has helped you.
* Think of a time when you have felt that God was very close to you. If you like, you can share this with the group.

Activity

❖ In pairs: imagine one person is Eli and one Hannah and have a conversation about what has happened and how you felt about it. Talk about what kind of boy Samuel might be.

 Play 'The story of Samuel' lotto game or cut and separate symbols to sequence for a storyboard.

B. In the Bible, prophets were men or women who spoke God's word for the people. They encouraged people and also reminded them about living God's way. Zephaniah was a prophet. Listen to what Zephaniah was saying: God's Story 3, p.67. Ask the children to look at the text in their Activity book.

Some questions to wonder about

* What does Zephaniah tell us about God?
* What surprised you and why?
* How does this passage of scripture make you feel?

Activity

❖ This is God speaking to you. On a postcard send God a text reply.

Activity book

Talk about the page in the Activity book.

Reflect and connect

 A prayerful moment. We thank God for his great love and delight in us. Pray together the words of Zephaniah.

*'The Lord your God is with you.
The Lord will take delight in you.
And in his love he will give you new life.
He will sing and be joyful over you.'*

Or the prayer of Hannah

*'I am so happy.
God has done great things for me.
I am so happy for God has helped me.
God's name is holy.
There is no-one like God.
God is so very good.
God is always near.'*

Sing: '*My God loves me*', (ICYF-CD1 / AYOC 149).

Autumn Theme 1 | Session 3

SESSION 3:
Families
God who never stops loving

Before you begin

Reflect on what this means to you:

'Let the peace of Christ rule in your hearts, to which indeed you were called in the one body and be thankful.'

Colossians 3:15

From the Catechism of the Catholic Church, 2205:

The Christian family is a communion of persons, a sign and image of the communion of the Father and the Son in the Holy Spirit.

This is what you are trying to communicate

God desires that every family reflects the loving unity that can be seen in the relationship of Father, Son and Holy Spirit. By living in this way we give God praise and joy.

How we might go about it

You will need

- ❊ PRAYER FOCUS with: a cloth, candle, icon/picture of the Holy Family.
- ❊ Pictures of a variety of families.
- ❊ Pictures of an outline of a cake headed: 'Recipe for a Happy Family'.
- ❊ God's Story 3, p.141: *'Be real about loving.'* Have copies of this for each child.
- ❊ Have a cake that could be shared at the end of the session. (Check if any children have allergies; e.g. nuts, gluten etc.)

Welcome and gathering

Have a short moment of silence. While the candle is lit, make the Sign of the Cross. Listen to the words from the letter to the Romans, God's Story 3, p.141: *'Be real about loving'* (the first sentence only) and say together our family prayer, the Our Father... Sing a song thanking God for our families.

Let's remember

Ask the children to remember the last session, share/discuss the page in the Activity book from the previous session. They may recall:

- ❊ The people who bring them joy in their lives.
- ❊ God's joy and delight in them.
- ❊ How they share that joy with others.

Let's share

Think about families. Our families are the people we live with; those who love and care for us. They come in all sorts of shapes, sizes and cultures. Show the children pictures of different sorts of families. Adapt these pictures to suit the children in your group.

Some questions to wonder about

* What is the best thing about families?
* What do families enjoy doing together?
* What are the things you have to work at to make a family happy?

Let's discover

We have all been made by God who loves us, and takes joy in us. God wants us to be happy and know that we are loved. We belong to God's family as well as our own human family. Jesus was also part of a human family. Sometimes it is not easy to be really loving. Listen to the advice St Paul gives for a Christian family: God's Story 3, p.141 (based on Romans 12:8-11). It might be a good idea to have copies of this text for children. Allow time for the children to think about the text quietly by themselves.

Activities

* Share the following questions in two or three or in a whole group. Keep notes of what the children say.

Some key questions to wonder about

* Which line did you like best in that advice and why?
* Which part of the advice do you think is most important for you and why?

Activities

* Whole group activity: Suggest that the children do this in 2's or 3's if numbers allow. What would you include in a recipe for a happy family? (e.g. 500 grams of forgiveness etc. 10 kind words). Build up the recipe together on a cake shape.
* Talk about each group's recipe.

 Use symbol supported text pack for cake recipe; play the 'Doing things with my family' lotto game.

 Use symbols of family members to choose verses for 'Thank you' songs.

 Use rich tea biscuits and icing pens to make happy faces of family members.

Activity book

Talk about the page in the Activity book.

Reflect and connect

Start with a prayerful moment thanking God for our families. Invite the children to name a member of their family whom they would like to pray for. After each petition the group responds by saying "Lord in your love, hear our prayer" or a short sung response (ICYF-CD4/CFE 542). Think quietly of how you will contribute to the recipes for happiness in your family. Sing: *'If you're happy and you know it clap your hands...'*

Now share the cake and remember that Jesus wants us to be happy and have fun together.

Don't forget

Be sensitive in talking about families and be aware of different kinds of family and their social backgrounds.

Remind the children to bring any photos of their Baptism to the next session.

Autumn Theme 2

BELONGING | BAPTISM | SACRAMENT

Baptism: We all want to belong.
God loves us so much that through the Sacrament of Baptism
God invites us to belong to the Church family.

SESSION 4:
Called

Baptism, a new life

Before you begin

Reflect on what this means to you:

'I pray that Christ will make his home in your hearts through faith. I pray that you may have your roots and foundation in love.'

Ephesians 3:17

From the Catechism of the Catholic Church, 1229:

'From the time of the apostles, becoming a Christian has been accomplished by a journey and initiation in several stages... certain essential elements will always have to be present: proclamation of the Word, acceptance of the Gospel entailing conversion, profession of faith, Baptism itself, the outpouring of the Holy Spirit.'

This is what you are trying to communicate

An understanding of Baptism as a call to a new way of life.

You will need

- PRAYER FOCUS with: a cloth, some symbols of Baptism, holy water, candle, white garment, shell, some oil, God's Story 3, music: *'Come and join the circle'*.
- Church's Story 3, pp.40-43.
- Large candle shapes, with either of the words 'l-i-g-h-t' or 'c-a-l-l-e-d' written down the side.

Leader's Book 2 — Autumn Theme 2 | Session 4 | 29

How we might go about it

Welcome and gathering

Have a short moment of silence. While the candle is lit, make the Sign of the Cross using the holy water. Listen to St Paul in God's Story 3, p.141: 'Be real about loving.'

Sing the song 'Come and join the Circle' from the 'Share the Light' CD by Bernadette Farrell.

Let's remember

Ask the children to remember the last session. Share/discuss the page in the Activity book from the previous session. They may recall:

* Recipes for a happy family.
* God wants us to be happy together and know that we are loved.

Let's share

When we choose to join a club or group, we usually do if for a good reason. It affects us in some way. We give something to the group and we receive something.

Some questions to wonder about

* Who belongs to a club or a society or a special group at school?
* How did you join, who invited you?
* What kind of difference has it made to you to belong to that club/group?

Let's discover

As well as belonging to our families and to the groups we have been talking about, everyone here belongs to the Church family.

Show pictures from Church's Story 3, pp.38-43 and share the pictures the children have brought in. If you were baptised as a baby, your parents and godparents made promises to help you to grow up to love God and everyone else. When children who are your age are baptised, they make promises themselves to love God and everyone else. You were given a candle to symbolise the light of Christ in your life. Through Baptism you have been called to keep the flame of faith alive. On Easter night, whilst holding a lighted candle everyone renews again the promises which were made at their Baptism.

Some questions to wonder about

* Why do you think there is a gospel reading at Baptism?
* At Baptism what kind of life are you called to live?
* What might help you?
* Every Sunday at Mass we say aloud what we believe, can you remember when we do that and some of what we say?

Activity

❖ On the candle shape use each letter to make up a sentence, poem or prayer about living in the light of Christ.

 Sort and stick activity using symbols packs, 'Groups I belong to,' 'Rules and promises,' 'Living like Jesus.'

Activity book

Talk about the page in the Activity book.

Reflect and connect

Gather round the prayer focus and have a bowl of holy water and a lighted candle. Invite each child to dip their finger in the water and slowly make the Sign of the Cross and say the words "In the name of the Father..." When we do this, we remember that we are baptised members of the Church family. Sing from 'Share the light' CD Bernadette Farrell 'You have called us by our name' or 'Baptised in Water', (ICYF-CD4 / CFE 67).

SESSION 5:
Confirm

Confirmation: a Sacrament to strengthen the baptised person's relationship with God and the Church

Before you begin

Reflect on what this means to you:

'There is one body and one Spirit, just as there is one hope to which God has called you. There is one Lord, one faith, one baptism; there is one God and Father of all, who is Lord of all, works through all, and is in all.'

Ephesians 4:4-6

From the Catechism of the Catholic Church, 1303:

...Confirmation brings an increase and deepening of baptismal grace: ...it gives us a special strength of the Holy Spirit to spread and defend the faith by word and action as true witnesses of Christ.

You will need

- ❀ PRAYER FOCUS with: cloth, candle, God's Story 3.
- ❀ Church's Story 3, pp.44-49,
- ❀ God's Story 3, p.109.
- ❀ If you choose to do the 'stained glass window', you will need a roll of greaseproof paper, felt tip pens, some cotton wool and olive oil.
- ❀ Invite teenage guests who have been recently confirmed.

This is what you are trying to communicate

Confirmation: a Sacrament to strengthen the baptised person's relationship with God and the Church.

How we might go about it

Welcome and gathering

After the candle is lit, take a short quiet moment "*In the name of the Father...*". Read '*The Promise of the Spirit*' from God's Story 3, p.109. Pray: '*Come Holy Spirit fill the hearts of your faithful and enkindle within them the fire of your love.*' Sing: '*All over the world*', (ICYF-CD1 / AYOC 112).

Let's remember

Ask the children to remember the last session, share/discuss the page in Activity book from the previous session. They may recall:

- ✱ How belonging to a group or club affects you.
- ✱ How Baptism calls us to live in the light of Christ.

Let's share

There are times when we all need support and help.

Some questions to wonder about

* Has anyone ever helped you when you had difficulty?
* How were you supported?
* Think of someone you have helped. How did you support them?

Let's discover

In the last session we talked about how you became a member of the Church's family. Confirmation strengthens and 'confirms' us in our relationship with God and the Church. Many people are baptised when they are babies and confirmed when they are older. The Sacrament of Confirmation is celebrated during the parish mass. It is usually the bishop who confirms. (You may need to talk about the words you have used) Look at Church's Story 3, pp. 44-49, explain the main parts of the rite of Confirmation. The oil of chrism (a sweet smelling oil) is also used at Baptism and Ordination.

Activities

A. In twos or threes, design a 'stained glass window' showing the symbols of Confirmation e.g. tongues of fire, dove, oil, mitre, crosier, laying on of hands and ring. Designs can be drawn on greaseproof paper, which is then coated in olive oil to make it transparent (N.B. make sure the children's clothes are protected).

B. Introduce the teenage guests who are to be interviewed about their experience of Confirmation. (If it is not possible to find recently confirmed young people, it is still good to bring in an adult who can be questioned.)

Activities cont.

❖ Make sure the young people are well prepared beforehand by giving them the questions which the children will ask them. Let them take turns to ask the young people these key questions and any other questions they may have:
  - How did you get ready for Confirmation?
  - What name did you choose and why?
  - Who was at your Confirmation?
  - Where did it take place?
  - What happened?
  - What did you promise?
  - Who helps you to keep these promises?

N.B. In Church's Story 3, p.46. The text states: *'A person who chooses to be confirmed promises to live as a Christian and follow the teaching of Jesus with the help of the Holy Spirit.'*

Activity book

Discuss the pages in the Activity book. Two activities are offered, **A** and **B**.

 Use 'Confirmation' and 'Pentecost' lotto games for matching, story board or cut and stick activity.

Reflect and connect

Gather round the prayer focus and read from God's Story 3, p.144 – from Paul's letter to the Galatians. The newly confirmed might like to help with the reading.

Pray: *'Come Holy Spirit'*.

Sing: *'Walk in the Light'*, (ICYF-CD3 / AYOC 198) or *'We are one in the Spirit'*, (ICYF-CD3 / AYOC 122).

SESSION 6:
Life choices
Christian life; marriage, ordination

Before you begin

Reflect on what this means to you:

'There are different ways of serving, but the same Lord is served.'

1 Corinthians 12:5

From the Catechism of the Catholic Church, (Christian Holiness), 2013: All Christians in any state or walk of life are called to the fullness of Christian life and to the perfection of charity. [Lumen Gentium 40] 'All are called to holiness.' 1534: ...Holy Orders, and Matrimony are directed towards the salvation of others; if they contribute as well to personal salvation, it is through service to others that they do so. They confer a particular mission in the Church and serve to build up the People of God.

You will need

- ❋ PRAYER FOCUS with: white cloth, candle, wedding ring, stole, chalice, paten and holy oil.
- ❋ Church's Story 3, pp.20-23 and pp.72-83.

This is what you are trying to communicate

Baptism and Confirmation are the beginning of the journey of the Christian vocation. The Christian life is expressed in a variety of ways including marriage and ordination, which have their own special sacraments. Remember to stress that that God is also served equally by those who remain single and those in religious life.

How we might go about it

What follows provides ample material from which the catechist needs to select according to the age group of the children and their ability. This could also be used over a two-year period or different material with different groups.

Welcome and gathering

Have a short quiet moment, then, whilst the candle is lit, make the Sign of the Cross. Read from St Paul's letter to the Colossians 3:10-11 (God's Story 3, p.147).

You might sing *'God made me as I am'* from 'Share the Light' CD by Bernadette Farrell or *'Oh Living Water'*, (ICYF-CD4 / CFE 566).

Let's remember

Ask the children to remember the last session, share/discuss the page in the Activity book from the previous session. They may recall:

* How we support each other in times of difficulty.
* What happens at Confirmation?
* How Confirmation helps us in our daily life.

Let's share

Some questions to wonder about

* What do you dream about doing when you are grown up? Why?

Think of an adult whom you admire because of the good they do for other people. Who are they? Take turns to tell everyone about them.

Let's discover

Activity

❖ Using copies of the pictures from Church's Story 3, pp.22-23 or other pictures cut them out and give to the children. Ask them what each person is doing and how they might be showing their love for Jesus.

A: Marriage

Now we are going to explore a special way God calls people to share the mission of Jesus through marriage.

Some questions to wonder about

* Who has been to a wedding in church?
* What did you think was most important during that wedding?

If possible, ask a recently married couple to talk to the children briefly about their marriage ceremony in Church. Use the following prompts: What happens at the ceremony? What would you say is the most important part of the ceremony and why? E.g. promises made by the couple in the presence of God and the priest and their family and friends. Use Church's Story 3, pp.74-77 to illustrate this. Show the wedding ring and talk about what it means: a sign of faithful love because it has no end.

Using Church's Story 3, pp.72-73, think about:

* What would you see?
* What would you hear?
* Who might be there?
* What will be happening?

(It is important to be sensitive to the reality that some children may come from a family where their parents are not married.)

 Engage the children with some of the many multi-sensory items associated with wedding celebrations, eg. bubbles in wedding cake and champagne bottle shaped containers, musical wedding cards, mini disco balls/lights etc.

B: Ordination

Ordination is a sacrament which celebrates the gift of priesthood and life and friendship with God the Father, with Jesus and one another. A priest chooses to give his life for the service of others in Church. This is his response to God's call to live a life filled with love for God's people. (Be aware of the different situations of priesthood e.g. married former Anglicans).

Ask a priest or deacon to come to be interviewed by the children about his ordination, particularly emphasising the laying on of hands (remember the laying on of hands at Confirmation). If this is not possible use Church's Story 3, pp.78-79.

Ask him to talk about his life as a priest or a deacon (the deacon needs to explain his particular mission). Encourage the children to ask questions.

 Bring in vestments for children to see and feel.

Activity book

Talk about the page in the Activity book.

Reflect and connect

 Gather round the prayer focus and read from Church's Story 3, p.21 (last two paragraphs).

Compose a 'litany-type' prayer for the different ways in which people are called by God to carry out the mission of Jesus e.g.

For Mums and Dads who love us and care for us...
   We thank you, Lord.

For those who teach us at school...
   We thank you, Lord.

For bishops, priest and deacons...
   (Perhaps name them)
   We thank you, Lord.

For those preparing to get married...
   Please help them Lord.

For those preparing to be priests...
   Please help them, Lord.

For those who share their food with the hungry...
   We thank you, Lord.

For those who visit the sick and the lonely...
   We thank you, Lord etc

In pairs, ask the children to lay hands on each other and pray for them.
Encourage them to do this slowly and prayerfully.

Sing: '*Give me joy in my heart*', (ICYF-CD4 / CFE 190).

Autumn Theme 3

LOVING – ADVENT
CHRISTMAS – CHRISTIAN LIVING

The Church's year: Advent /Christmas, the birth of Jesus, God so loved the world that He sent His only Son to earth as a person. We prepare for and celebrate that love during Advent and Christmas.

SESSION 7:
Birthdays
Looking forward to Jesus' birthday

Before you begin

Reflect on what this means to you:

'For a child has been born for us, a son given to us; authority rests upon his shoulders; and he is named wonderful Counsellor, Mighty God, everlasting Father, Prince of Peace.'

Isaiah 9:6

From the Catechism of the Catholic Church, 437: From the beginning he was 'the one whom the Father consecrated and sent into the world,' conceived as 'holy' in Mary's virginal womb. God called Joseph to 'take Mary as your wife, for that which is conceived in her is of the Holy Spirit,' so that Jesus, 'who is called Christ', should be born of Joseph's spouse into the messianic lineage of David.

This is what you are trying to communicate

Advent and Christmas: the Church's seasons for preparing for and celebrating the birth of Jesus

You will need
- PRAYER FOCUS with: purple cloth, Advent wreath and candles.
- Church's Story 3, pp.86-88: Isaiah 35.
- Pens.
- Coloured pencils.

36 | Autumn Theme 3 | Session 7 | Leader's Book 2

How we might go about it

Welcome and gathering

 Take a quiet moment to reflect. Light the appropriate numbers of candles on the Advent wreath and make the Sign of the Cross. Say a word or two about the meaning of the wreath, the circle and the candles.

Say the prayer:

> 'God our loving Father,
> we thank you for giving us Jesus to be the light in our darkness.
> Bless us as we gather in his name,
> and bless this wreath
> as a sign of his light among us.'

Sing an Advent song, or a candle song e.g. 'Light the Advent candle', (ICYF-CD2 / AYOC 49).

Let's remember

Ask the children to remember the last session, share/discuss the page in the Activity book from the previous session. They may recall:

* Their ideas for what they want to do when they grow up.
* Something about the sacraments of marriage and/or ordination.

Let's share

Some questions to wonder about

* Think about a special birthday
* Whose birthday was it and why was it very special?
* How did you celebrate?
* What do birthdays tell us about ourselves?
* How do we prepare to celebrate something special?

Let's discover

Whose special birthday are we preparing for now in Advent?

Every year when we are waiting to celebrate the birthday of Jesus at Christmas we remember how the Jewish people waited for hundreds and hundreds of years for the Promised One they called the Messiah. Through the prophets, who were men or women who spoke God's word to the people, they knew that God promised to send a special person who would bring healing and peace and fairness to the world. He would come from the family of their great King David.

Isaiah was a prophet who lived a very long time before Jesus. We still read his words in church in Advent because they help us to get ready to welcome Jesus. Isaiah describes what will happen when the Messiah comes. Listen carefully and see if you can remember the one detail you like best.

Listen to the words of Isaiah from Church's Story 3, p.88, 'When the Messiah comes', (based on Isaiah 35).

 **Some questions to wonder about**

* Does this remind you about Jesus in any way?
* What story about Jesus does this reminds you of?

Activities

A: During Advent we have the time and opportunity to prepare for the coming of Jesus at Christmas by doing something special each day, such as saying a special prayer or doing good for someone. In pairs, share ideas and then begin to fill in the Advent calendar in the Activity book.

B: Have you heard about family trees? How we track our ancestors, our grandparents and great grandparents. We can build up a family tree. Jesus was born into a human family; he had ancestors. We know the family story of Jesus from what we have learnt from the Old Testament.

Activities continued

During Advent we think about the faithfulness of God encouraging his people to prepare for Jesus the Messiah to come and live with us. In Isaiah 11:1 we read: 'A shoot will spring forth from the stump of Jesse, and a branch out of his roots.' That shoot was Jesus. Draw a Jesse tree in the Activity book and add symbols to it.

> 🙂 Assemble a Jesse tree and a story bag of multi-sensory items linked to life and story of Jesse tree people. Do a turn-taking song using an array of symbol/picture choice cards, passing around a picture of baby Jesus to 'Which of Jesus' family shall we hear about (today?)' (Tune: 'Here we go round the mulberry bush') Help the child holding the picture at the end of each verse to choose a character to match to the one on the tree and animate the associated story with items from the bag.

Let's share

Activity book: Talk about the page in the Activity book – the Advent calendar/ Jesse tree.

Reflect and connect

✝ Gather round the prayer focus, light the candle on the Advent wreath and put the work done in the session in front of the prayer focus. Ask each child to read out the line they like best from Isaiah, pausing between each.

Say the prayer again:

> 'God our loving Father,
> we thank you for giving us Jesus
> to be the light in our darkness.
>
> Bless us as we gather in his name,
> and bless this wreath
> as a sign of his light among us.'

Sing an Advent song or a candle song, e.g. 'Light the Advent candle', (ICYF-CD2 / AYOC 49).

Resources

Mission Together, Missio usually produce an Advent calendar, as does CAFOD in its primary section.

SESSION 8:
Hope

Waiting in joyful hope for Jesus, the Promised One, the Messiah

Before you begin

Reflect on what this means to you:

> 'For God loved the world
> so much that he gave his only Son.'
>
> John 3:16

From the Catechism of the Catholic Church, 422:
'But when the time had fully come, God sent forth his Son born of a woman...' God has visited his people. He has fulfilled the promise made to Abraham and his descendants. He acted far beyond all expectation – he has sent his own 'beloved Son'.

You will need

- PRAYER FOCUS with: purple cloth, Advent wreath and candles.
- Globe or map of the world.
- CAFOD resources for Advent, God's Story 3, p.95, or a large poster with the prayer from the preface of Advent II:

    'In his love Jesus has filled us with joy
    As we prepare to celebrate his birthday
    So that when he comes
    He may find us watching in prayer
    Our hearts filled with wonder and praise.'

- A large sheet of paper with the word H O P E in the centre and some post-it notes.

This is what you are trying to communicate

The prophets told the people of the *Promised One*, who was to come, and the need to prepare for him.

How we might go about it

Welcome and gathering

Have a quiet moment to reflect. Light the appropriate numbers of candles on the Advent wreath and make the Sign of the Cross.

'God our loving Father,
we thank you for giving us Jesus
to be our hope.

Bless us as we gather in his name
and bless this wreath
as a sign of his hope among us.'

Sing an Advent song or a candle song e.g. *'Light the Advent candle'*, (ICYF-CD2 / AYOC 49).

Let's remember

Ask the children to remember the last session. Share/discuss the page in the Activity book from the previous session. They may recall:

* How and why we celebrate special birthdays.
* How we prepare for the coming of Jesus at Christmas.

Let's share

Talk for a moment about what the word 'hope' means to each person. Let them write their ideas on a post-it note and stick it round the word 'hope' on the big sheet.

Some questions to wonder about

* What is your deepest hope, one that would make others happy? (the catechist might give an example. Remember that 'hope' is not the same as 'wishing.' If you wish, then you do not have to do anything. If you hope, you need to work to bring it about.)
* How could we realise our deepest hope?

Let's discover

The prophet Isaiah was writing when the people of Israel were going through a difficult time after their country had been invaded by a powerful enemy. His greatest hope was that the Messiah, the Promised One, would come and change people's lives for the better. Jesus used Isaiah's words when he stood up in the synagogue and told people what he had come to do. Read: *'Jesus begins his mission'* from God's Story 3, p.95, (based on Luke 4). This is Jesus' mission. During Advent as we await the birth of Jesus we think about the hope he brings and how it inspires us to bring hope to others.

Some questions to wonder about

* What hope does Jesus bring us?
* Who do you think are in need of hope in our world today? Make use of the world map or the globe or a CAFOD poster and see if the children can tell you where there are people in need of peace or help etc.

Activities

* Using either the CAFOD or Missio materials, arrange some activities based on offering hope to others round the world or in their home parish.

> Cut and stick activity with Widgit symbols 'How we bring our hope in Jesus to others' using symbol sentence strips denoting ways of offering help and support.

* He's got the whole world in His hands' song activity. Form a circle and throw inflatable globe ball to each other. At the end of each verse child/adult chooses symbol card to decide next verse, eg. He's got people who are hungry in His hands, repeat until all have a turn.

* **Activity book:** Talk about the page in the Activity book.

Reflect and connect

Gather round the prayer focus, the candles on the Advent wreath and have a quiet moment to reflect on the work of the session. Say together the prayer in the Activity book from the preface of Advent or:

*'God our loving Father,
we thank you for giving us Jesus
   to be our hope.
Bless us as we gather in his name,
and bless this wreath as a sign
   of his hope among us.'*

Sing an Advent song, or a candle song e.g. *'Light the Advent candle'*, (ICYF-CD2 / AYOC 49).

Don't forget

Talk about what will happen next week.

SESSION 9:
Expectation
Jesus was born to show God to the world

Before you begin

Reflect on what this means to you:

'And God showed his love for us by sending sent his only Son into the world so that we might have life through Him.'

1 John 4:9

From the Catechism of the Catholic Church, 458: The Word became flesh so that thus we might know God's love.

You will need

- PRAYER FOCUS with: purple cloth and an Advent wreath.
- God's Story 3, p.105, (the first paragraph of 'Finding Jesus').
- A small wrapped gift for all children and adults.
- Crayons and pencils and some paper in case the Activity book is forgotten.
- Small crib and figures.
- Food for the party.

This is what you are trying to communicate

Advent and Christmas: the Church's seasons of preparing to receive and celebrate with joy and gratitude God's gift of love made known in Jesus.

How we might go about it

Welcome and gathering

Have a quiet moment to reflect as the candles of the Advent wreath are lit.

Sing the Advent hymn, '*Come Lord Jesus*', (ICYF-CD4 / CFE 128).

Sing an Advent song, or a candle song e.g. '*Light the Advent candle*', (ICYF-CD2 / AYOC 49).

*'God our loving Father,
we thank you for giving us Jesus to be our joy.
Bless us as we gather in his name,
and bless this wreath as a sign of his joy among us.'*

If possible play the song '*Prepare ye the way of the Lord*' from the CD of the musical GODSPELL, or sing the Taizé chant: '*Prepare the way of the Lord*', (ICYF-CD4 / CFE-612, 904).

Leader's Book 2 — Autumn Theme 3 | Session 9 | 41

Let's remember

Ask the children to remember the last session, share/discuss the page in the Activity book from the previous session. They may recall:

* Their greatest hope for the world.
* Jesus and the hope he brought to everyone.

Let's share

Some questions to wonder about

* Talk about something you have been promised and are expecting.
* What do you do whilst you are waiting?
* Have you ever promised someone something?
* Have you always kept your promise and why?

Let's discover

God always keeps his promises.
Explain who Jesus' cousin, John the Baptist, was. Recap briefly the Visitation of Mary to Elizabeth. John was the last prophet before Jesus was born. He helped to prepare the people for Jesus, the Promised One.
Listen to the reading from St John's gospel about how John describes Jesus. Read God's Story 3, p.105 the first paragraph of *Finding Jesus.*

* What name does John give to Jesus?
* What do you think it means?
* What does he tell us about why Jesus came to earth?

In St Luke's gospel we hear John the Baptist telling people how to prepare for the coming of Jesus.

What are we to do?

(Based on Luke 3:10-16)

You may dramatise this story with the children.

* * *

When people asked John the Baptist what they must do, he said, "You must share with each other. If you have two coats, give one to someone who has no coat at all. Give food to those who are starving."

Some tax collectors asked him, "What are we to do?"

"Don't collect more money than you should," he told them.

Some soldiers also asked him, "What about us? What are we to do?"

He said to them, "Don't bully people into giving you money. Be happy with your wages."

Everyone was excited. They began to think John might be the Christ for whom they were waiting. John said, "Someone more powerful than I am will come soon. I am not good enough to undo his sandals. He will bring you God's Spirit of love."

* What ideas did John have?
* What ideas do you have?

Play 'The Visitation' and/or 'John the Baptist' lotto games.

Activity book

Talk about the page in the Activity book.

Reflect and connect

Join the younger group for their Nativity play or if there is no younger group sing some carols around the crib as you gradually put the figures in the crib. Distribute the gifts and have a little party.

Don't forget

Check allergies if you are having food.

Spring Theme 4

OUR STORY
THE COMMUNITY OF FAITH
LOCAL CHURCH

Community – Local Church: We not only belong to our families we also belong to the local community – to our parish and our diocese. We come together as a community to celebrate important times of the year in the Church as well as important events in our lives.

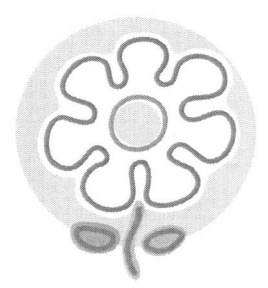

SESSION 10:
Books
God's Story for the Church family

Before you begin

Reflect on what this means to you:

> 'Seeing that many others have undertaken to draw up accounts of the events that have taken place among us, exactly as these were handed down to us by those who from the outset, were eyewitnesses and ministers of the word, I in my turn, after carefully going over the whole story from the beginning, have decided to write an ordered account for you.'
>
> Luke 1:1-2

From the Catechism of the Catholic Church, 104:
'In Sacred Scripture, the Church constantly finds her nourishment and her strength, for she welcomes it not as a human word, "but as what it really is, the word of God." In the sacred books, the Father who is in heaven comes lovingly to meet his children, and talks with them.'

This is what you are trying to communicate

For Christians the Bible is very special. The Bible is the story of God's love, told by the People of God and how the people have responded to that love. Readings from the Bible are used in church on Sunday by the parish family. The Gospels teach us about Jesus and his mission.

Leader's Book 2 — Spring Theme 4 | Session 10 | 43

You will need
- ✿ PRAYER FOCUS with: a Bible, candles, music.
- ✿ God's Story 3; Church's Story 3, pp.56-57; if possible some Good News Bibles.
- ✿ A basket of prepared readings suitable for varying abilities and ☺ some Widgit symbols taken from the texts used in the activities. The cards could be in the shape of a Bible.
- ✿ Three sheets of paper, one headed 'Old Testament', one 'New Testament – Letters,' one 'New Testament Gospel'. The titles of which are to be sorted, written on individual pieces of paper.

How we might go about it

Welcome and gathering

Have a short moment of stillness, then the Bible flanked by candles, is carried in procession and placed on the focal point. An Alleluia is sung during this time. Make a Sign of the Cross on the forehead, saying "God be in my mind," a Sign of the Cross over the lips, saying "God be on my lips," and a Sign of the Cross over the heart, saying "God be in my heart." Use the following psalm for the prayer.

> 'Come, my children. Listen to me.
> Who loves to be happy all the time?
> Who enjoys having good times together?
> Well, so does God!
>
> God cares for you.
> God knows what you want.
> God listens.'
>
> Based on Psalm 34

Let's remember

Ask the children to remember the last session, share/discuss the page in the Activity book from the previous session.

- ✱ Keeping promises.
- ✱ Jesus the one Promised by God, stories of Christmas.

Let's share

Some questions to wonder about

- ✱ What are your favourite kind of books and why? (Mystery, fairy tales, poetry, history, factual books...)
- ✱ How do you find books you want in the library? (At school or the public library)
- ✱ How do you treat books and why?

Let's discover

We have a special book called the Bible, which we hear read in church. The collection of Bible readings is in a book called The Lectionary (the Bible is in fact a library of books).

Let's look at the Bibles we have brought in. Look at the list of contents in the front, what do you notice? See if you can find a book in the Old Testament? See if you can name a book in the New Testament?

Use Church's Story 3, pp.56-7, which illustrates the 'Liturgy of the Word' at Mass.

Some questions to wonder about

- ✱ When do we hear the Bible being read?
- ✱ Who does the first reading?
- ✱ What do we do?
- ✱ What does the reader of the Gospel do before he reads and why?
- ✱ What do we do when we listen to the Gospel at Mass and why?

Using Church's Story 3, pp.56-57, talk about how at Sunday Mass the first reading is usually from the Old Testament and the second reading is usually from one of the letters in the New Testament and the third reading is always from the Gospel.

Activities

Have three sheets of paper one headed 'Old Testament', one 'New Testament – Letters,' one 'New Testament Gospel'.

A. Invite the children in pairs to sort the following titles and place them on the right sheet of paper where they belong:

- The story of Jesus' birth.
- Letter to the Hebrews.
- The Crucifixion.
- Moses and the Ten Commandments.
- The Prodigal Son.
- Letter to the Philippians.
- The call of Samuel.
- The story of Creation.

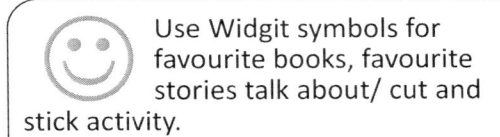

> Use Widgit symbols for favourite books, favourite stories talk about/ cut and stick activity.

B. Here is a list of readings from the Old and New Testaments. Look them up in the Good News Bibles. (Explain what the numbers mean, e.g. the chapter and the verses)

- Luke 2:1-7; Genesis 1;
- Luke 15: 11-32;
- Matthew 27:45;
- Philippians 1:12-17;
- 1 Samuel 2-3;
- Exodus 20:1-17;
- Psalm 139.

Activity book

Look together at the tasks in the Activity book.

Reflect and connect

Gather round the prayer focus, have a moment of silence.

Share this ritual of reverence for the Bible by singing an alleluia (ICYF-CD4 / CFE 410) to greet the gospel and say with gestures: *'God be in my mind, God be on my lips and God be in my heart.'*

Have a short gospel reading, e.g. Luke 2:22-39 (God's Story 3, p.78).

Place the Bible on the prayer focus and finish by all singing an alleluia.

Don't forget!

Remind the children to listen carefully to the readings at Mass or in the Children's Liturgy.

For the next session

Catechists: if your parish has a website, a printout of ministries would be useful. Organise some key parishioners to act as panellists in the next session.

Leader's Book 2 Spring Theme 4 | Session 11 | 45

SESSION 11:
My parish

Life in the local Christian community – the parish

Before you begin

Reflect on what this means to you:

'We are God's work of art, created in Christ Jesus to live the good life as from the beginning he had meant us to live it.'

Ephesians 2:10

From the Catechism of the Catholic Church, 905:
'Lay people fulfil their prophetic mission by evangelisation, which is the proclamation of Christ by word and the testimony of life.'

This is what you are trying to communicate

The parish is a Christian community in a geographical area. A parish church is where the community gathers. Everyone has their part to play in the community.

How we might go about it

Welcome and gathering

Have a short moment of stillness, with some music or a bell. Whilst the candle is being lit, make the Sign of the Cross. Place a Bible in a central position.

Read from Mark 3: 13-14 or from God's Story 3, p.90 I have chosen you, the first paragraph.

Sing: 'We are his people', (CFE 984) or 'The People of God' (Moses, I know you're the man), (ICYF-CD2 / AYOC 126).

Let's remember

Ask the children to remember the last session, share/discuss the page in the Activity book from the previous session. They may recall:

* Books are part of our lives. They have lots of uses.
* We read and listen to the Bible in Church.

You will need

* PRAYER FOCUS with: a candle and some photographs of parish life.
* Church's Story 3, pp.24-25. Use some photographs of parish activities.
* A copy of the parish newsletter.
* Map showing parish boundaries. (The resource 'Celebrate Together', Rejoice Publications, ISBN 978-1-899 48-126-2, is very good on this topic.)

Let's share

Some questions to wonder about

* What kind of things do you enjoy doing together as a family or a class in school?
* How does that help you enjoy each other's company?

Let's discover

(We need to recognise that parishes are places where people gather but the geographical area may vary.)

* What is the name of the Church where we worship?
* What are some of the activities (social and maintenance) that happen in our Church?
* Who is involved and what are the age groups?
* How do these activities help build the Church community?
* Who looks after our church? Talk about the people in the photographs and the jobs they do in the church.
* Does anyone else use part of our Church e.g. the hall?

Parish is the name given to a Christian community in a certain area.

Activity

* Prepare some questions for the people in the parish.
* Set up a panel of the priest and involved parishioners and ask them your questions.

Match Widgit symbols to photographs to create poster of people and their jobs in the Parish.

Activity book

Talk about the activity in the Activity book.

Reflect and connect

Gather round the prayer focus.
Sing: 'Children of God in one family', (ICYF-CD1 / AYOC 137) or 'We are his people', (CFE 984) or 'Though we are many' from Share the Light CD by Bernadette Farrell.

Compose a litany of thanks for the people and the work they do for the parish using the response 'We praise and thank you, Lord.'

Invite the children to complete the phrases and add to them.

>For our priest who…
>
>For our deacon who…
>
>For our parish catechists who…
>
>For our readers who…
>
>For our…

Don't forget!

Prepare a map of the diocese. Bring to the next session any information you can find about your diocese.

SESSION 12:
My Diocese
Continuing Jesus' mission

Before you begin

Reflect on what this means for you:

'In our prayers for you we always thank God, the Father of Our Lord Jesus Christ for we have heard of your faith in Christ Jesus and of the love you have for all the saints, because of the hope laid up for in heaven'

Colossians 1:3

From the Catechism of the Catholic Church, 833:
...the diocese refers to a community of the Christian faithful in communion of faith and sacraments with their bishop ordained in apostolic succession.

You will need

- ❀ PRAYER FOCUS with: God's Story.
- ❀ Pictures of Jesus, the Good Shepherd, and the local Bishop (if possible showing the bishop with mitre, cross and crosier).
- ❀ Church's Story 3, pp.26-27.
- ❀ A sheet with pictures of a mitre, crosier, ring and cross or a bishop wearing these.
- ❀ An enlarged copy of the diocesan coat of arms.

This is what you are trying to communicate

An understanding of the diocesan community, the bishop and those who help him in continuing Jesus' mission.

How we might go about it

Welcome and gathering

Have a short moment of stillness, with some music or a bell. Whilst the candle is being lit, make the Sign of the Cross.

Listen to the story of the '*Good Shepherd*' from God's Story 3, p.104.

After a time of reflection, invite the children to say something from the story about the shepherd or the sheep.

Song: '*The Light of Christ*' (ICYF-CD3 / AYOC 83).

Let's remember

Ask the children to remember the last session, share/discuss the page in the Activity book from the previous session. They may recall:

- ✻ The activities they do as a family or class and how these help them to become a family or a class.
- ✻ How people work together to build the parish community.

Let's share

Some questions to wonder about

* What is the name of your teacher at school?
* What does he or she do?
* What is the name of your head teacher?
* How does he or she help the children and help the teachers?

Let's discover

Use Church's Story 3, pp.26-27 to explain what a diocese and a bishop are. A diocese is made up of many parishes. The Bishop leads the Christian family. The main church of the diocese is called a 'cathedral', where the Bishop presides for important celebrations.

Share the facts they have found out about their diocese.

Look at a picture of your bishop, the coat of arms and talk about the geography of your diocese.

Some questions to wonder about

* What is the name of our bishop?
* What does the coat of arms tell you about your bishop and the diocese?
* What do you notice about him, what is he wearing and what is he carrying?
* What similarities do you notice between the Good Shepherd and the Bishop?
* What similarities are there in their responsibilities?

Talk about the bishop's mitre, his hat, and the two points of it representing the Bible and the Church. The cross which he wears around his neck shows that he walks in the footsteps of Christ. The ring shows he is faithful to God and to leading his people, (just as married people wear wedding rings.) The crosier is like a shepherd's crook and is a symbol his service to the community as leader or shepherd.

His role is to lead and support all the parish families and unite them as Catholics. He celebrates the Sacrament of Ordination and usually the sacrament of confirmation. His mission is to proclaim the Gospel and the priests and the deacons in the parishes help him in this.

Bishops are the successors of the apostles. The first bishop was St Peter.

Activity

A. Give out the sheets with the picture of the bishop or the symbols he wears and ask the children to say what each means.

> Play 'The Good Shepherd' lotto game and/or do 'All about our Bishop' collage activity using Diocesan newspaper cuttings and Widgit symbols.

B. Think about the questions they would like to ask their Bishop. Use these to write a letter to their Bishop for the catechist to send to him.

Activity book

Talk about the page in the Activity book.

Reflect and connect

Gather round the prayer focus. Have a moment of stillness with music or a bell.

Reflect on the picture of the Good Shepherd and the photograph of the Bishop, remembering that the bishop is the Good Shepherd of the Diocese.

Repeat each line after the Catechist:

> 'Strengthen in faith and love, your pilgrim Church on earth,
>
> your Servant Pope Benedict,
>   our Bishop …and all the bishops
>
> with the clergy and the entire people
>   your Son has gained for you.
>
> Father, hear the prayers of the family
>   you have gathered here before you.
>
> In mercy and love unite all your children
>   wherever they may be. Amen'

Spring Theme 5

| EUCHARIST | RELATING | SACRAMENT

Eucharist – Relating: We find strength in gathering for the celebration of the Eucharist, a sign of God's love in our lives. We share memories, love and thanks as we celebrate the life, death and resurrection of Jesus and receive him in Holy Communion.

SESSION 13:
Thanksgiving
Thanksgiving for Jesus

Before you begin
Reflect on what this means for you:

> 'While they were eating, he took a loaf of bread, and after blessing it he broke it, gave it to them and said, "Take; this is my body." Then he took a cup, and after giving thanks he gave it to them, and all of them drank from it. He said to them, "This is my blood of the covenant, which is poured out for many."'
>
> Mark 14:22-24

From the Catechism of the Catholic Church, 1360:
'The Eucharist is a sacrifice of thanksgiving to the Father, a blessing by which the Church expresses her gratitude to God for all his benefits, for all that he has accomplished through creation, redemption and sanctification. Eucharist means first of all "thanksgiving." '

This is what you are trying to communicate

The Eucharist: the Church's prayer of thanksgiving.

You will need
- *PRAYER FOCUS* with: a coloured cloth according to the liturgical year, candle, Bible as well as a loaf of bread, wheat, grapes and a bottle of wine.
- Pictures of nature, different images of people, some icons [pictures] of Jesus and Jesus' death and resurrection, glue and large sheets of paper.
- A copy of the Children's Eucharistic prayer 1: Preface, Holy, holy and the first paragraph after that, which can be pasted into the Activity book.

How we might go about it

Welcome and gathering

Have a short moment of stillness, with some music or a bell. Whilst the candle is being lit, make the Sign of the Cross. Have a few moments of silence while we think what we want to thank God for today.

Read part of 'An Early Christian Hymn' from God's Story 3, p.145, ('*Give thanks to God...*').

A gathering hymn with a thanksgiving theme, for example, '*We really want to thank you, Lord*', (ICYF-CD3 / AYOC 33) or '*Thank you for giving me the morning*', (ICYF-CD3 / AYOC 10) or some similar hymn of thanksgiving.

Let's remember

Ask the children to remember the last session, share/discuss the page in the Activity book from the previous session. They may recall:

* The people who make up our diocese.
* The bishop who is the leader of our diocese.

Let's share

Think quietly for a moment about the good things in your life you want to say thank you for.

Some questions to wonder about
* Why are we thankful?
* Who has made you happy?
* Who have you made happy?

Let's discover

We have many things to be thankful for. Before we have a meal at home, perhaps we say a prayer thanking God for our food. We call this 'grace before meals.'

The Eucharistic Prayer. The word Eucharist means 'thanksgiving' and at each Mass, the greatest meal, we have a special prayer of thanksgiving, which we call the Eucharistic Prayer. Paste the Children's Eucharistic Prayer 1 into the Activity book and look at it together.

Some questions to wonder about
* Which words do you like best in that prayer and why?
* Can you think of one great thing God has done for us?
* What does this prayer tell us about Jesus?

Activity

A. Choose a picture that reminds you of that prayer, say why, and put it on a large sheet.

> Do a 'thank you' song activity. Let the children choose each verse for, 'If you're happy and you know it, thank the Lord.' eg. for 'Mums and Dads,' 'food and drink,' 'hamsters and rabbits,' 'Jesus in the bread,' 'Jesus in the Wine,' etc. (Use Widgit symbol pack)

B. Write your own prayer of thanksgiving.

Activity book

Together look at the page on *Thanksgiving*.

Reflect and connect

Gather round the prayer focus, have a few quiet moments to reflect on the session, say together a few phrases from the Children's Eucharistic Prayer that sum up the work you have done together.

Sing or say the 'Holy, holy' or say part of the Gloria from the Mass ('*Peruvian Gloria*', ICYF-CD4 / CFE 198), a great prayer of thanksgiving.

Don't forget

Remind the children to bring a photo or object next week that has special significance for their family. It might be a picture of their First Holy Communion.

Leader's Book 2 Spring Theme 5 | Session 14 | 51

SESSION 14:
Memories

The Eucharist, the living memorial of Jesus

Before you begin

Reflect on what this means for you:

> 'For I received from the Lord what I also handed on to you, that the Lord Jesus on the night when he was betrayed took a loaf of bread and when he had given thanks, he broke it and said, "This is my body that is for you. Do this in remembrance of me".
> 'In the same way he took the cup also, after supper, saying', "This cup is the new covenant in my blood. Do this, as often as you drink it, in remembrance of me." '
>
> 1 Corinthians 10:23-25

From the Catechism of the Catholic Church, 1364:
'In the New Testament, the memorial takes on a new meaning. When the Church celebrates the Eucharist, she commemorates Christ's Passover, and it is made present: the sacrifice Christ offered once for all on the Cross remains ever present. "As often as the sacrifice of the Cross by which 'Christ our Pasch has been sacrificed' is celebrated on the altar, the work of our redemption is carried out." '

Bring to mind stories from your own life that somehow make persons or events of the past present to you now.

This is what you are trying to communicate

The Eucharist keeps the memory of Jesus alive and makes him present with us in a special way.

You will need
- *PRAYER FOCUS* with: a coloured cloth according to the liturgical season, candle, lectionary or a Bible.
- A family photo.
- If possible, the song '*Memory*' from the musical 'CATS' or any other song which includes memories.
- Some hymn books.

How we might go about it

Welcome and gathering

Have a short moment of stillness, with some music or a bell. Whilst the candle is being lit, make the Sign of the Cross.

Play the song '*Memory*' from the musical 'CATS' CD.

Read: '*What I heard, I am handing on*' from God's Story 3, p.143.

Let's remember

Ask the children to remember the last session, share/discuss the page in Activity book from the previous session. They may recall:

* Things for which they are thankful.
* Something from the Children's Eucharistic Prayer.

Let's share

Talk about the objects/photos/card/letter which the children have brought in and ask them, if they wish, to explain why it has a special significance for them. (*Take care, as this may be a sensitive area for some children**)

As leader, you may wish to share something of your own which evokes a special family memory.

A good book to read is '*Wilfrid Gordon McDonald Partridge*' by Mem Fox, published by Puffin, ISBN 978-014050-586-3 or *Badger's Parting Gifts* by Susan Varley, published by Collins Picture Lions, ISBN 978-000664-317-3.

Let's discover

The Christian family kept the memory of Jesus alive as he had asked them to do by celebrating the Eucharist as a living memory of him. This is how St Paul explains it in his letter to the people who were living in Corinth.

Read from 1 Corinthians 11: 24-27, or read '*What I Heard, I am Handing on*' from God's Story 3, p.143.

Some questions to wonder about

* What is the special memory of Jesus that Paul is writing about?
* What do you remember of the story?
* What does Paul say they are doing when they eat this bread and drink this cup?
* When do we take part in this special remembrance of Jesus?

Activity

* Invite the children to role play the Last Supper. As they are doing it, talk about what they want to remember of that experience and what it means to them.

  > Use Widgit 'Holy Communion' book which links actions of Jesus and friends at Last Supper to actions of priest and people at Mass.

  > Use Last Supper/Mass lotto for matching or storyboard activity.

Activity book

Talk about the page in the Activity book.

Reflect and connect

Gather round the prayer focus and play the song, '*Memory*' from the CD again. Quietly say a prayer to thank Jesus for his presence in Holy Communion.

Don't forget!

*Take care when sharing memories, some memories may be quite sad and if necessary refer to the parish guidance on dealing with abuse and bereavement.

Leader's Book 2   Spring Theme 5 | Session 15 | 53

SESSION 15:
Unity

The Eucharist enables people to live in communion

Before you begin

Reflect on what this means for you:

> 'When you are offering your gift at the altar, if you remember that your brother or sister has something against you, leave your gift there before the altar and go: first be reconciled to your brother and sister and then come and offer your gift.'
>
> Matthew 5:23-24

From the Catechism of the Catholic Church, 790:
'Believers who respond to God's word and become members of Christ's Body become intimately united with him: "In that body the life of Christ is communicated to those who believe, and who, through the sacraments, are united in a hidden and real way to Christ in his Passion and glorification."'

You will need

- ❃ *PRAYER FOCUS* with: a coloured cloth according to the liturgical year, candle, Bible as well as loaf of bread, wheat, grapes, a bottle of wine.
- ❃ Pictures of a crowd shopping and a football crowd.
- ❃ A football scarf, shirt etc.
- ❃ Two large pieces of paper with 'communion' and 'community' written on them.
- ❃ Coloured markers.
- ❃ A4 sheets with the following heading printed on them: 'At Mass Jesus helps us to live in communion by...'
- ❃ Make sure that everyone has enough glue and scissors, etc.

This is what you are trying to communicate

The Eucharist challenges and enables us to live and grow in unity with God and each other every day.

How we might go about it

Welcome and gathering

Have a short moment of stillness, with some music or a bell. Whilst the candle is being lit, make the Sign of the Cross.

Sing: 'We are one in the Spirit', (ICYF-CD3 / AYOC 122) or 'One Bread one body,' or 'Though we are many' from 'Share the Light' CD by Bernadette Farrell.

Introduce the Our Father as the Church's family prayer. Say it prayerfully together.

Let's remember

Ask the children to remember the last session, share/discuss the page in the Activity book from the previous session. They may recall:

- ✶ A special memory.
- ✶ At Mass we remember the life, death and resurrection of Jesus.

Let's share

Look at the pictures of a crowd shopping and a football crowd. What is the same and what is different about the people in the pictures? Look at the scarf and the shirt, talk about them.

Some questions to wonder about

* What does it feel like to support a team or be a member of a team?
* What brings people together?
* What is good about coming together as a group?
* How can you keep the unity in a group?

Let's discover

Hold up two large pieces of paper with the words 'Communion' and 'Community' written on them. Talk about these words and highlight the two separate and different words at the end of 'Communion' and 'Community'.

Some questions to wonder about

* Does anybody know what the word communion means?
* Another word like communion is community. What do you think this word means?
* What other words are are at the end of these words? ('union', 'unity')
* Talk about what union and unity means. Discuss ways that enable us to live together in communion (putting others first).
* Talk about how Communion means 'being at one with'. In the celebration of the Eucharist the Christian family becomes more at one with Jesus, with God the Father and the Holy Spirit, and with one another.
* Talk about gathering together, listening to the Word of God, sharing our belief, (the Creed), praying the Our Father, sharing the Sign of Peace, receiving Jesus in Communion, sending out to love and serve the Lord.

Activity

* In small groups design a poster with a heading "At Mass Jesus helps us to live in communion by..." and an illustration and some phrases to show how we might do that. (It might be a good idea to ask if these posters could be put up in church.)

Use Widgit symbol supported text sentences to ensure above activity is accessible; sing the circle song below, tying together long length of rope or ribbon so that everyone in the circle can hold on and feel the strength of the ribbon when pulled.

Sing: *'We are strong when we're together* (x3)
living in communion'

(Sung to the tune of the traditional nursery song: *Bobby Shaftoe*, or do the same song with parachute activity, taking it in turns for child to sit under while others lift it up and down.

Reflect and connect

Gather round the prayer focus. Pray together the prayer for peace and unity that we hear at Mass after the Our Father or the prayer '*Lamb of God...*'

Have a few quiet moments reflecting on how they can bring peace and unity in their families and with their friends.

End with giving each other the sign of peace.

Activity book

Talk together about the page in the Activity book.

Spring Theme 6

GIVING | LENT/EASTER | CHRISTIAN LIVING

Lent/Easter – giving: we all learn to grow by trying to follow what is good and rejecting what is bad, choosing life over death. This often means we have to be generous and self-giving like Jesus. Easter celebrates Jesus' resurrection: the victory of life over death, good over evil. You will be exploring this with the children in three sessions: Giving all, Self-discipline and Death and New Life.

SESSION 16:
Giving all

Lent is a time to remember Jesus' total giving

Before you begin

Reflect on what this means to you:

> 'For even the Son of Man did not come to be served; he came to serve and to give his life to redeem many people.'
>
> Mark 10:45

From the Catechism of the Catholic Church, 2099: It is right to offer sacrifice to God as a sign of adoration and gratitude, supplication and communion: 'Every action done so as to cling to God in communion of holiness, and thus achieve blessedness, is a true sacrifice.'

This is what you are trying to communicate

Introduce the season of Lent. Introduce the idea of using the time to think about the sort of giving we are involved in.

Spring Theme 6 | Session 16

You will need

- *PRAYER FOCUS* with: a purple cloth; candle; picture of the Washing of the Feet; large jug of water, bowl and towel; background music on CD.
- Church's Story 3, pp.96-98, God's Story 3, p.115.
- Sufficient cards for everyone to write a Lentern promise on.
- A Lenten calendar (see Missio www.missio.org.uk or CAFOD www.cafod.org.uk websites) which may be useful.

How we might go about it

Welcome and gathering

Have a short moment of stillness, with some music or a bell. Whilst the candle is being lit, make the Sign of the Cross.

Introduce the season of Lent as a time to think about giving.

Sing: '*Give me yourself*', (ICYF-CD4 / CFE 192).

Jesus gave his friends a very clear sign of the way they should give. Read John 13:34-35.

Jesus said:

> "I am giving you a new rule for living;
> love one another.
> You must love one another in the same way as I have loved you.
> If you do this, every one will know that you are my friends,
> and God's friends too."
> Amen.

Let's remember

Ask the children to remember the last session, share/discuss the page in the Activity book from the previous session. They may recall:

- What keeps a team together?
- How Jesus helps us to live in communion with Him and with others.

Let's share

Some questions to wonder about

- Have you ever found it difficult to share something that was very special to you? And why?
- Have you ever had to give something up to help someone else?
- What has been good about sharing and giving?

Let's discover

Talk about what happened on Ash Wednesday and what the ashes signify and the words 'Repent and believe the Gospel.' (see Church's Story 3, pp.96-98).

Why do we have purple cloth?

During Lent there are no 'alleluias' sung in church and no flowers. Talk about Lent as the opportunity for changing ourselves which is why we focus on prayer, fasting (giving up something) and giving to each other. Discuss ideas for doing some of these on a regular basis during Lent.

Jesus was always ready to give a good example to others and show them how to give to each other and not try to be important.

Just before the Last Supper Jesus got a bowl of water and a towel and washed his disciples' feet. Explain to the children the significance in Jesus' time of the lowly task of the servant washing the feet of the guests and why it was necessary to wash people's feet in that country at that time. Ask the children if anyone has seen this happen at church on Maundy Thursday?

Read God's Story 3, p.115 based on John 13: 4-9, 12-15.

Activities

- Mime the story without using water or without asking children to take off their socks. The catechist could give the example and then enable the children to act out the story together of the servant and the guest.

  ### Some questions to wonder about

  * How did it feel to mime washing someone's feet?
  * How did you feel when someone pretended to wash your feet?
  * How did Jesus' friends feel when He washed their feet?
  * Why did Peter not want his feet washed?
  * We can serve each other in different ways. How can we do this, in home, at school, among our friends?

  > Play Maundy Thursday lotto.

- Make a Lenten promise card.

Activity book

Discuss the page in the Activity book.

Reflect and connect

Gather round the prayer focus. They may like to read out their Lenten promises.

After each promise repeat the refrain:
'Help us to do as Jesus did and love one another.'

Sing: *'Give me yourself'*, (ICYF-CD4 / CFE 192).

SESSION 17:
Self discipline
Celebrating growth into new life

Before you begin

Reflect on what this means to you:

'God is always at work in you to make you willing and able to obey his own purpose.'

Philippians 2:13

From the Catechism of the Catholic Church, 540:
'...For we have not a high priest who is unable to sympathise with our weakness, but one who in every respect has been tested as we are, yet without sinning. By the solemn forty days of Lent the Church unites herself each year to the mystery of Jesus in the desert.'

You will need

- PRAYER FOCUS with: a desert scene (sand, stones, dry twigs), Bible, purple cloth.
- If possible a CD with the sounds of nature (blowing wind, etc.).
- Paper and pens.

This is what you are trying to communicate

Lent is an opportunity for renewing our growth in self-discipline.

How we might go about it

Welcome and gathering

Have a short moment of stillness, with some music or a bell. Whilst the candle is being lit, make the Sign of the Cross.

Play some 'nature' music and invite the children to look at the focus. Remind the children that Lent is an opportunity to grow in holiness, to grow in God's way, and to choose between bad and good.

Sing: *'Father I place into your hands'*, (ICYF-CD4 / CFE 159).

Let's remember

Ask the children to remember the last session, share/discuss the page in the Activity book from the previous session. They may recall:

- About sharing and giving.
- Their Lenten promises.
- Jesus washed the feet of his friends.

Let's share

* Some questions to wonder about
* What do you need in your life to stay healthy?
* What do you give up or not do in order to keep healthy?
* When do you have to be self-disciplined?
* What helps you?

Let's discover

During Lent Christians pray to gain understanding and strength to recognise good and bad. Lent is a time when Christians practice self-discipline in order to grow in God's way. We give or make sacrifices as an expression of our love for God and for one another.

Talk about what self-discipline means in our lives; e.g. it is necessary to have it when we cross a road, to live peacefully with others etc.

Sometimes we are tempted to do what we know is not right or good. Like us, Jesus was tempted but he always chose to do good.

Listen to the story of Jesus' temptation in the desert.

Read: *'Jesus Chooses God's Way'*, from God's Story 3, p.94.

Some questions to wonder about

* What does the story about Jesus in the desert tell us about his choices in a difficult situation?
* Who did Jesus put first when he was tempted? Why?
* How does the example of Jesus help you to overcome your temptations?

Activity

* Make a chart: one column has a list of things that you find difficult; the other column has the choices you can make to be more like Jesus. Choose three where you will try to put others first this Lent.

  Use Widgit symbols to cut and stick for the 'Being more like Jesus' activity.

  Play the 'Being good/Doing wrong' lotto game; Do the 'Being good/Doing wrong' 'cut and stick' activity with symbols.

Activity book

Talk about the page in the Activity book.

Reflect and connect

Gather round the prayer focus. Bring your chart and in silent prayer ask Jesus to help us to have the strength and courage to have the self-discipline to be faithful to the choices we have made for this Lenten season.

Say together a prayer of St Francis (*'Make me a channel of your peace'*) from your Activity book.

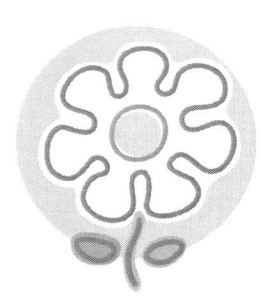

SESSION 18:
Death and New life
Celebrating Jesus' death and Resurrection

Before you begin

Reflect on what this means to you:

'If the Spirit of him who raised Jesus from the dead is living in you, then he, who raised Jesus from the dead, will give life to your own mortal bodies through his Spirit living in you.'

Romans 8:11

From the Catechism of the Catholic Church, 638:
'We bring you the good news that what God promised to the fathers, this day he has fulfilled to us their children by raising Jesus. The Resurrection of Jesus is the crowning truth of our faith in Christ.'

You will need

- ❀ PRAYER FOCUS with: a purple cloth, candles, crucifix, maybe a picture of the one the Stations of the Cross for the prayer focus.
- ❀ Church's Story 3, pp.100, 104-109, God's Story 3, p.112, 118 ff.

This is what you are trying to communicate

Holy Week and Easter remembering and celebrating Jesus' suffering and death that leads to new life.

How we might go about it

Welcome and gathering

Have a short moment of stillness, with some music or a bell. Whilst the candle is being lit, make the Sign of the Cross.

Sing the Taizé chant *'Jesus remember me'*, or *'I met you at the Cross'*, (ICYF-CD2 / AYOC 88) or something similar.

Read: *'The Soldiers'*, from God's Story, p.118 (based on Mark 15: 16-21) or read it from the Bible.

Say together:

> 'Lord, by your cross and resurrection, you have set us free.
> You are the Saviour of the World.'

Let's remember

Ask the children to remember the last session, share/discuss the page in the Activity book from the previous session. They may recall:

- ❋ How we need self-discipline in our lives.
- ❋ How Jesus dealt with temptation.

N.B. *Before reading the 'Let's share' section, check that no one in the group has lost a significant person in their life from death or separation.*
If so, change this text to something about seeds being buried in the ground before they fruit.

Let's share

Talk about the loss of someone, perhaps a friend who has moved away, or a grandparent who has died or a pet.

The leader might tell a brief story of their own experience of loss or read a book like *'Little Bear's Grandad'* by Nigel Gray (published by Little Tiger Press, ISBN 1-85430-637-5).

Sometimes people we love move away, go into hospital or a person or a pet may die.

Some questions to wonder about

* How did you feel when this happened to you?
* What helped you?
* Do you sometimes talk about them?
* In what ways are they still there for you?

Let's discover

During Holy Week and Easter the Church tells the story of the suffering, death and resurrection of Jesus that leads to new life. The sadness of loss leads to a new and different joy.
Talk about how the statues are covered in purple cloth to remind the Church family of the 'dying' in order to celebrate the new life of Easter.

The last three days of Holy week are called the Easter Triduum, that is: Maundy Thursday, Good Friday and Holy Saturday (Church's Story 3, p.100).

Remind the children about Jesus washing the feet of the disciples and how we remember that on Maundy Thursday.

Set the scene of Good Friday when Jesus was arrested, tried and crucified (God's Story 3, p.118 or Church's Story 3, page 104).

Activities

❖ Explain about the Stations of the Cross. If possible go to the church and look at them. Choose two or three to pray at. If your church has a 15th station of the Resurrection, include that in your prayers.

❖ Read God's Story 3, p.120 and 122 or p.123.

Some questions to wonder about

✲ What happened on the way to Calvary?
✲ How do you think Simon felt?
✲ What do you think about this?
✲ Who was Jesus thinking about when he was on the Cross?

> Use Widgit 'Easter Story' to sequence events of Holy Week and Easter, match key symbols to the corresponding page in the story.

> Play 'Good Friday' lotto game.

All the gospel writers tell us that 3 days after Jesus died he rose again.
We celebrate that on Easter Sunday.

Activity book

Talk about the page in the Activity book

Reflect and connect

Gather round the prayer focus, sing the Taizé chant, *'Jesus remember me'* or *'Father, we adore you'*, (ICYF-CD1 / AYOC 114) or something similar.
Pray the prayer:

> 'We adore you, O Christ,
> and we bless you,
> because by your holy Cross,
> you have redeemed the world.'

or something similar.

Summer Theme 7

Serving in love | Pentecost | Christian living

Pentecost – Serving: People respond to belonging to a community by telling others about it, being witnesses of its values, and by having an energetic and lively commitment to it every day of their lives. Pentecost celebrates the gift of the Holy Spirit who empowers the Church to proclaim the Good News.
For followers of Jesus, every day is a holy day.

SESSION 19:
Energy
Gifts of the Holy Spirit

Before you begin

Reflect on what this means to you:

'You will receive power when the Holy Spirit has come upon you: and you will be my witnesses in Jerusalem, in all Judea and Samaria.'

Acts 1:8

From the Catechism of the Catholic Church, 735:
'...This love is the source of new life in Christ, made possible because we have received 'power' from the Holy Spirit.'

This is what you are trying to communicate

Pentecost: the Holy Spirit gives the friends of Jesus new energy to use for their good and the good of others.

You will need
- *PRAYER FOCUS* with: a gold or red coloured cloth, God's Story.
- Candle, torch, batteries.
- Church's Story 3, p.113.
- Gifts of the Spirit written on separate large sheets of paper: 'wisdom', 'understanding', 'right judgement', 'courage', 'knowledge', 'reverence and wonder' and 'awe in God's presence'.
- Flame-shaped pieces of coloured paper for each child and felt pens.

How we might go about it

Welcome and gathering

Have a short moment of stillness, with some music or a bell. Whilst the Paschal candle is being lit, (explain briefly that this reminds us about the light of the Risen Jesus), make the Sign of the Cross. Pause and ask the children, "who do we name thirdly when we make the Sign of the Cross?"

Read: Acts 1:6-11 (God's Story 3, p.132), *The Ascension*.

Say this prayer together, '*Come Holy Spirit fill the hearts of your faithful and enkindle within them the fire of your love. Amen*'.

Sing: '*All over the world*', (ICYF-CD1 / AYOC 112).

Let's remember

Ask the children to remember the last session, share/discuss the page in the Activity book from the previous session. They may recall:

* How it feels when we lose someone.
* The death and Resurrection of Jesus.

Let's share

Have you ever wondered what energy is? Everything needs energy to live and move and function. Perhaps you have learnt about energy at school in science lessons. What do you know about it?

Some questions to wonder about

* What energy does the light in the room need? (Electricity)
* What energy does a torch need to work? (Use the torch with and without batteries)
* What gives you energy?
* Have you ever helped someone to do something that they have not got the energy to do? How did you help them?

Let's discover

Read from Church's Story 3, p.113, how the disciples felt dejected and without energy when they thought they were alone and how the gift of the Holy Spirit gave them the energy and power to spread the Good News of God's love. We also need this special energy and the gifts it brings.

Some questions to wonder about

* How do you think Jesus' friends felt about their task of bringing Good News of God's love to the world when Jesus left them?
* What kind of help did they need? (Courage, understanding, confidence, strong love of Jesus, etc.)

Talk about the gifts of the Holy Spirit: e.g. *wisdom, understanding, good judgement, courage, knowledge, reverence* and *wonder and awe in God's presence* and what they might mean.

Activities

* Give out a flame shape to each child and ask them to choose one of the gifts of the Holy Spirit and write it on the flame and say how they think that gift can help them and others.
* Ask the children to form into small groups. Ask each group to choose a gift and describe a situation where this might be needed. Then ask the each group to take turns to tell the whole group which gift they chose and why.

Play 'Pentecost' and/or 'Gifts and Fruits' Lotto games. Use 'Gifts' symbol supported text sentences to do flame shape activity.

Activity book

Talk about the page in the Activity book.

Reflect and connect

Gather round the prayer focus and ask for the gifts we need.

Sing: '*Spirit of the Living God*' or '*All over the world*', (ICYF-CD1 / AYOC 112).

SESSION 20:
Transformation
Celebrating the Spirit's transforming power

Before you begin

Reflect on what this means to you:

'The Advocate, the Holy Spirit whom the Father will send in my name will teach you everything.'

John 14: 26

From the Catechism of the Catholic, 735:
This is the source of the new life in Christ, made possible because we have 'power' from the Holy Spirit.

You will need
* *PRAYER FOCUS* with: gold or red cloth, Paschal candle, Good News Bible.
* God's Story 3, pp.132.
* Large sheets of paper labelled 'before' and 'after'.

This is what you are trying to communicate

The Holy Spirit can change us as the first apostles were changed.

How we might go about it

Welcome and gathering

Have a short moment of stillness, with some music or a bell. Whilst the candle is being lit, make the Sign of the Cross.

Say this prayer together: *'Come Holy Spirit fill the hearts of your faithful and enkindle within them the fire of your love. Send forth your spirit and you shall renew the face of the earth. Amen.'*

Sing: *'Abba Father send your Spirit'*, (ICYF-CD1 / AYOC 111).

Let's remember

Ask the children to remember the last session, share/discuss the page in the Activity book from the previous session. They may recall:

* Needing energy for various tasks.
* Pentecost: the coming of the Holy Spirit on the apostles and Mary.
* The Gifts of the Holy Spirit.

Let's share

Think about the ways you have changed in the last five years? You are the same person but you have developed new skills. We can all change. (The catechist could give an example.)

Some questions to wonder about

* What can you do now that you could not do five years ago?
* Where did you learn those skills?
* How long did it take you?
* How have you used these skills?

Let's discover

The friends of Jesus also experienced a change when the Holy Spirit came.

Talk about how they felt before the Holy Spirit came (read: God's Story 3, p.132).

Some questions to wonder about

* What happened to the people on Pentecost morning?
* What did the people notice about the apostles?

Every year we keep the birthday of the Church on the feast of Pentecost (see: Church's story 3, p.113). We can invite Jesus' Spirit every day to help us change and become more and more alive. The gifts of the Holy Spirit can help us and those gifts can produce fruit. If we use the gifts then with practice we can be transformed/changed and begin to have more love, joy, peace, patience, kindness, goodness, faithfulness, gentleness and self-control. Look at the page in the Activity book.

Activities

* In bigger groups make two living pictures, that is a *frozen* tableau of the two scenes, 'before' and the 'after' of Pentecost. Alternatively draw the scenes on large sheets of paper labelled 'before' and 'after'.

> Use Widgit symbols to 'choose and stick' to ensure the above activities are accessible for all the children.

> Sing: 'Spirit of the Living God fall afresh on…………..' (say child's name) whilst blowing bubbles over them each in turn.

* Make a birthday card for the Church, telling it what gifts it has received from Jesus' Spirit.

Activity book

Talk about the page in the Activity book.

Reflect and connect

Gather round the prayer focus.
Sing: *'Abba Father, send your Spirit'*, (ICYF-CD1 / AYOC 111).

Take it in turns to say: *'Thank you Holy Spirit for the gift…'* (whatever gift the children choose, not necessarily the official ones). Make the Sign of the Cross slowly, remember we are signed with the Holy Spirit.

SESSION 21
Witness

The Holy Spirit enables people to become witnesses

Before you begin

Reflect on what this means to you:

> 'Peter standing with the eleven, raised his voice and addressed them, "Men of Judea and all who live in Jerusalem, let this be known to you and listen to what I say… This Jesus, God raised up and of that all of us are witnesses."'
>
> Acts 2:14, 32

From the Catechism of the Catholic Church, 738:
'In her (the Church) whole being and in all her members, the Church is sent to announce, bear witness, make present and spread the mystery of the communion of the Holy Trinity.'

You will need

- PRAYER FOCUS with: gold or red cloth, Paschal candle, Good News Bible (Acts 2:32-39).
- Large sheet of paper and pens.
- God's Story 3.

This is what you are trying to communicate

How Jesus' friends spread the message of the Good News of Jesus at Pentecost.

How we might go about it

Welcome and gathering

Have a short moment of stillness, with some music or a bell. Whilst the candle is being lit, make the Sign of the Cross.

Pray together:

> 'Come Holy Spirit
>   fill the hearts of your faithful
> and enkindle within them
>   the fire of your love.
> Send forth your Spirit
>   and you shall renew the face of the earth. Amen.'

Sing: 'All over the world', (ICYF-CD1 / AYOC 112).

Let's remember

Ask the children to remember the last session, share/discuss the page in the Activity book from the previous session. They may recall:

* How we can all change.
* How the Holy Spirit transformed the apostles and can transform us.

Let's share

What is another word for witness (Spectator, observer, onlooker)? Have you ever been a witness to something, perhaps someone receiving a prize or perhaps to someone being bullied? Think of a time when someone asked you what you saw.

Some questions to wonder about

* How did you feel?
* Was this difficult and, if so, why?

Let's discover

Read the story from Acts 2:32-39. The friends of Jesus were so full of the God's Holy Spirit that they could not stop telling everyone, witnessing, about Jesus.

Some questions to wonder about

* Why did Peter think it was important to tell the people about the Good News?
* How do you think Peter felt when he gave witness about Jesus to the people?
* What helped him?
* What was the result of his witness?
* It was through the courage of the witness of the apostles that we know about the love of Jesus.

Activities

A. In threes or more, imagine that one of you is an apostle and the other(s) wants to hear the Good News. What will the apostle say and how will the listeners respond?

Provide a selection of pictures/Widgit symbols for a 'choose and stick' poster activity. Choose a picture that shows people showing kindness.

B. Read together God's Story 3, p.134, 'The new people of God'. Talk about how the people acted and how you could apply those ideas today. Do you know anyone who lives like that? On a large sheet of paper make 2 columns, one entitled: 'Signs of new people' and the other: 'What it might mean for today'.

Activity book

Talk about the page in the Activity book.

Reflect and connect

Gather round the prayer focus. Listen to what the groups have to present.

Pray the opening prayer for the Mass of Pentecost:

> 'Let the Spirit you sent on your Church to begin the teaching of the Gospel, continue to work in the world through the hearts of all who believe. Amen'.

Sing: 'Make me a channel of your peace', (ICYF-CD2 / AYOC 147).

Summer Theme 8

SERVICE TO THE COMMUNITY
RECONCILIATION | SACRAMENT

Relationships bring joy and challenge. This means making choices, being open to change, taking responsibility for our actions and building bridges towards others. Christians try to follow Jesus' way of love. In the Sacrament of Reconciliation, the Church celebrates the gift of the love and mercy of God. It gives people strength and courage to confess sin, seek forgiveness and be reconciled to God and each other.

SESSION 22:
Choices

The importance of examination of conscience

Before you begin

Reflect on what this means to you:

'Since you have accepted Christ Jesus as Lord, live in union with him. Keep your roots deep within him, build your lives on him, and become stronger in your faith, as you were taught, and be filled with thanksgiving.'

Colossians 2:6-7

From the Catechism of the Catholic Church, 1776: 'Deep within his conscience man discovers a law which he has not laid upon himself but which he must obey. Its voice, ever calling him to love and do what is good and to avoid evil, sounds in his heart at the right moment.'

This is what you are trying to communicate

We have the opportunity to make choices; it is important that we choose wisely and try to live like Jesus.

You will need
- *PRAYER FOCUS* with: a table covered with a sand coloured cloth, a Good News Bible, candle, Cross, dish containing some pebbles and God's Story.
- God's Story 3, p.66 (*'Change!'*, Joel 2:12-13), God's Story 3, p.102/3.

Leader's Book 2 — *Summer* Theme 8 | *Session 22*

How we might go about it

Welcome and gathering

Have a short moment of stillness, with some music or a bell. Whilst the candle is being lit, make the Sign of the Cross. Read: '*Change!*', from God's Story 3, p66 (based on Joel 2:12-13). Glory be to the Father. Make the Sign of the Cross.

Let's remember

Ask the children to remember the last session, share/discuss the page in the Activity book from the previous session. They may recall:

* The experience of being a witness.
* How the apostles were witnesses to the Good News of Jesus.

Let's share

The catechist might like to tell a story from her own experience that illustrates the way in which we all have to make choices. Think of some of the choices you have made.

Some questions to wonder about

* How did you know whether it was a good or bad choice?
* What happened after the choice?
* Looking back, do you think you would make a different choice now, or would it be the same choice?
* Why

Let's discover

Christians try to live like Jesus lived. Many pray each day for the help they need to make wise choices. Before going to sleep each night it is good for us to 'examine our conscience'. This means that we think about the kind of person God wants us to be and the kind of things God wants us to choose. Thinking back on our day we remember the good choices we have made and say 'thank you' and for the bad choices we say 'sorry'. Talk about the children's experience of First Reconciliation.

Tell the story of the '*Prodigal son*' from God's Story 3, p.102/3 (based on Luke 15:11-32).

Some questions to wonder about

* What did the younger son choose to do?
* When did he realise he had made a bad choice?
* What choice did the older son make?
* Was he pleased to see his brother return?
* Do you think he was right?
* How did the Father feel about the younger son?
* Have you ever changed your mind about a choice you made? When and Why?

Activity

A. In a group re-enact the story.

> 😊 Use set circles or hoops and a selection of symbols/pictures for a sorting activity 'Good choices/bad choices' accompany with appropriate song to reinforce sorting, eg. '*Oh dear what can the matter be, somebody's……*'/somebody's helped their mum today Hooray! Hooray! (tune: '*The animals went in two by two*' to the tune of '*When Johnny comes marching home*').

> 😊 Use the 'Prodigal Son' lotto game for matching or storyboard activities.

B. Choose one of the sons from the Prodigal Son story. On a sheet of paper, make two columns. In the first, list the choices he made and in the second the consequences of the choices. Then consider your conclusions and these actions.

Continued ▷

Activity book

Talk about the page in the Activity book.

Reflect and connect

✝ Gather round the prayer focus. Give each child a pebble to hold and invite them to close their eyes and 'examine their conscience' by first thinking of the good choices they have made.

Together say a short 'thank you' prayer. Now ask the children to think of the bad choices they have made (and as they individually place their pebbles in the dish) together say a short 'sorry' prayer. Make the Sign of the Cross.

Make a storyboard showing the choices made by each of the Two Sons.

SESSION 23:
Building bridges

Admitting wrong, being reconciled with others and God.

Before you begin

Reflect on what this means to you:

> 'But now, in union with Christ Jesus you, who used to be far away, have been brought near by the blood of Christ.'
>
> Ephesians 2:13

From the Catechism of the Catholic Church, 1468: 'The whole power of the sacrament of Penance consists in restoring us to God's grace, and joining us with him in an intimate friendship.'

This is what you are trying to communicate

The importance of admitting wrong and being reconciled with each other and God.

You will need

- ❦ PRAYER FOCUS with: Table with cross and candle, cloth in the current liturgical colour (likely to be green) and cards.
- ❦ Cards, one for each child, with verses of ('*My love for you is great*') based on Hosea 11:1-4 in God's Story 3, p.67.
- ❦ God's Story 3, p.98 '*Jesus forgives a sinner.*'
- ❦ Paper, coloured pencils, glue.

Leader's Book 2 — *Summer* Theme 8 | Session 23 | 71

How we might go about it

Welcome and gathering

Have a short moment of stillness, with some music or a bell. Whilst the candle is being lit, make the Sign of the Cross.

Ask the children to read in turn, verses from their cards based on Hosea 11:1-4.

Sing: *'Will you come and follow me'*, (ICYF-CD4 / CFE 812) or another appropriate song, or listen to some music or say a prayer.

Make the Sign of the Cross.

Let's remember

Ask the children to remember the last session, share/discuss the page in their Activity book from their previous session. They may recall:

* The importance of making the right choices.
* The story of the Two Sons.
* The need to examine our consciences.

Let's share

What has been your experience of friendships? Sometimes there can be difficulties in the best of relationships.

Some questions to wonder about
* Can you remember a time when you fell out with a friend?
* What happened?
* Did you make friends again? When and how?
* Did you or your friend change in any way afterwards?

Let's discover

Making friends after falling out is like building a bridge in a broken relationship. This is called 'reconciliation'. Reconciliation with God means being truly sorry for the bad choices we have made. Listen to the story of the way Jesus forgives a sinner from God's Story 3, p.98 (based on Luke 7:36; 40; 44-50). Explain that: to the Pharisee anyone who did not keep God's law in every detail was a sinner. Simon was shocked to see Jesus accept this service from a woman who was known to be a sinner.

Some questions to wonder about
* Do you think this woman had made bad choices in her life?
* How did this woman make a bridge towards Jesus?
* Do you think she was sorry for the mistakes she had made in the past?
* What did Jesus tell the woman?
* What did Simon think?
* What was Jesus' response to Simon?

Activity

❖ Think quietly about a time when your friendship was broken with a friend. Write a prayer of reconciliation in the Activity book and decorate it.

Reflect and connect

Gather around the prayer table. Spend a few quiet moments before making the Sign of the Cross.

Say this prayer together based on love:

Love is always patient and kind.
It is never jealous.
Love is never boastful or conceited.
It is never rude or selfish.
It does not take offence and is not resentful.
Love takes no pleasure in other people's sins,
but delights in the truth.
It is always ready to excuse, to trust, to hope
and to endure whatever comes.
Love does not come to an end.
All the wonderful and clever things
that people can say and do will come to an end.
Love never ends.
Amen.

Spend a few moments in silent prayer.
Make the Sign of the Cross.

Don't forget!

Decorate your prayer of reconciliation and stick that and your prayer card into your Activity book.

SESSION 24:
Healing
The Sacrament of the Sick

Before you begin

Reflect on what this means to you:

> 'Are any of you ill? You should send for the church elders, who will pray for them and rub olive oil on them in the name of the Lord.'
>
> James 5:14

From the Catechism of the Catholic Church, 1527:
'The sacrament of Anointing of the Sick has as its purpose the conferral of a special grace on the Christian experiencing the difficulties inherent in the condition of grave illness or old age.'

You will need

- PRAYER FOCUS with: cloth in the current liturgical colour (likely to be green), a candle, a Good News Bible and prayer cards.
- Prayer cards with the prayer (see below).
- If possible, a poster or photograph of the anointing of the sick at Lourdes.
- Church's Story 3, pp.70-71, or any pictures of this Sacrament.
- Reading from the Good News Bible (Mark 2:1-12).

This is what you are trying to communicate

As Jesus had a special care for the sick and so do we. The Church through the prayer and anointing in this Sacrament continues the mission of Jesus for the comfort of the sick.

How we might go about it

Welcome and gathering

Have a short moment of stillness, with some music or a bell. Whilst the candle is being lit, make the Sign of the Cross.

Read the following prayer from the prepared prayer cards:

> 'Heavenly Father, at times we come into contact with people who need understanding... Sometimes it is hard to witness the suffering of those we are trying to comfort. Let your Holy Spirit be with us so that your love can speak through us. Amen.'

Spend a short moment in silent prayer for the people we know who are ill or suffering in any way.

Sing something like *'Lay your hands gently upon us'*, (CFE 347).

Make the Sign of the Cross.

Let's remember

Ask the children to remember the last session, share/discuss the page in the Activity book from the previous session.
They may recall:

* The importance of building bridges in broken relationships.
* Being able to admit and be sorry about wrong doing and be reconciled.

Let's share

Think about a time when you might have been ill, or when someone you have known and loved was ill. Perhaps you have been with someone who is suffering or afraid.

Some questions to wonder about

* What happened?
* How did you feel?
* What comforted you or the other person?

Let's discover

The Sacrament of the 'anointing of the sick' gives people the opportunity to celebrate God's gifts of hope, strength and healing. It brings people closer to God the Father, with Jesus and with one another. It brings comfort when people are suffering. The Church can sometimes be called 'the healing Church' because it brings the comfort and healing of Jesus Christ. Sometimes this sacrament is given to sick people in their homes or in hospital, sometimes in church during Mass and sometimes by the roadside or battlefield if someone is injured. Look at and talk about the pictures in Church's Story 3, (pp.68-71).

Some questions to wonder about

* What do you see in this sacrament?
* Who will be there?
* What happens?
* What will you hear?
* How do you think sick people and their friends and relations feel about this sacrament?

Activity

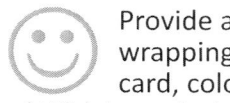

Provide a variety of stickers, wrapping papers, sparkly card, coloured tissue paper and Widgit symbols to make a get well prayer card for someone who is sick.

A. Make up your own prayer for a sick person.

B. Think about the last words of St Mark's Gospel; *'These are the signs that will be associated with believers... they will lay their hands on the sick, who will recover'* (Mark 16:17-18). Read how Jesus cures a paralytic man (Mark 2:1-12).

Questions to wonder about

* How was the paralytic man able to get close to Jesus?
* What were the first words Jesus said to him?
* What was the effect on those who were listening to him?
* What was the next thing Jesus said to the man?
* What happened?
* What do you think this story tells us?

Activity book

Talk about the page in the Activity book.

Reflect and connect

Gather round the prayer focus: Spend a few quiet moments thinking about those we know who are sick or experiencing difficulties of any kind and say a silent prayer for them or read out the prayer you have composed.
Now listen to a prayer called *'Christ Heals'*:

*'Everyone has some suffering and difficulty, it might be physical or it might be something we are afraid of or worried about.
There is always a healer and comforter. Jesus. He is close to you, he calls you his friend – prayer helps that friendship.
Amen.'*

Summer Theme 9

THE STORY
PEOPLE OF GOD
UNIVERSAL CHURCH

God created the world in all its richness and diversity. It is in our world that the story of God's love is experienced. We see the truth, goodness, and beauty of all creation, which is the glory of God. We all have the responsibility to reverence, respect, and care for God's gift.

SESSION 25:
Neighbours
Neighbours share God's world

Before you begin

Reflect on what this means to you:

'And now I give you a new commandment; love one another. As I have loved you, so you must love one another. If you have love for one another, then everyone will know that you are my disciples.'

John 13: 34-35

From the Catechism of the Catholic Church, 1825:
'The Lord asks us to love as he does, even our "enemies," to make ourselves the neighbour of those furthest away and to love children and the poor as Christ himself.'

This is what you are trying to communicate

Everyone is a neighbour loved by God and we are all connected.

You will need

- PRAYER FOCUS with: a rainbow cloth if possible, God's Story 3, p.100.
- Several 2-metre lengths of ribbon, enough for one per child, (florists' ribbon can be written on). Write a neighbourly act on each ribbon, a container for the ribbon.

How we might go about it

Welcome and gathering

Have a short moment of stillness, with some music or a bell. Whilst the candle is being lit, make the Sign of the Cross.

Read God's Story p.109 *'Jesus' prayer for his friends'* (the first part). Take a moment to pray for each other and those who are in special need.

Say: *'Glory be to the Father...'* etc.

Sing: *'Make me a channel of your peace'* (ICYF-CD2 / AYOC 147).

Let's remember

Ask the children to remember the last session, share/discuss the page in the Activity book from the previous session. They may recall:

* We try to comfort and help those who are sick.
* Something about the sacrament of the anointing of the sick.
* Jesus' healing ministry.

Let's share

Who are the neighbours you meet outside your family? Think about your neighbourhood, school, parish or a club you might belong to?

Some questions to wonder about

* Who lives next door to you?
* Who do you meet when you go out? e.g. church, shopping, clubs, the library.
* What visitors come to your school?
* What do you know about the people you meet?
* Where do they come from?

Let's discover

Tell the story of the *'Good Samaritan'* from God's Story 3, p.100 (based on Luke 10:25-37).

Some questions to wonder about

* Why did Jesus tell this story?
* How does it end?
* How did the teacher of the law answer Jesus' question?
* Would you agree with this and why?
* Did anything surprise you?
* How could you be a good neighbour in school? Can you think of a time when you have helped someone who was in trouble?

In threes, make up a story or use a real situation where someone is in trouble and another person is a good neighbour. Act it out for the group.

> Use 'Good Samaritan/Good Neighbour' lotto game for matching or storyboard activity.

Activity book

Talk about the page in the Activity book.

Reflect and connect

Gather round the prayer focus in a circle. Take time to think about how you can be a good neighbour to others and how we are all connected to each other. The leader or the children, take two ends of a ribbon, so that each will be connected with two other people (like a giant cat's cradle). Each child could read out the good deed on their ribbon, saying this week *'I will try to.......'* Sit down and put the ribbons on the floor.

Say God's family prayer together, *'Our Father...'*

Sing: *'When I needed a neighbour, were you there?'*, (ICYF-CD3 / AYOC 160) or something similar.

Next week: please bring in a picture of the country where you come from.

SESSION 26
Difference
Different saints show us what God is like

Before you begin

Reflect on what this means to you:

> 'We have many parts in the one body, and all these parts have different functions. In the same way, though we are many, we are one body in union with Christ, and we are all joined to each other as different parts of one body.'
>
> Romans 12:4-5

From the Catechism of the Catholic Church, 2013:
'Thus the holiness of the People of God will grow in fruitful abundance, as is clearly shown in the history of the Church through the lives of so many saints.'

You will need
- PRAYER FOCUS with: cloth, bible, candle a map of the world and God's Story 3.
- Images of local Saints e.g. patron saint of the parish, stories about saints (*Friends of Jesus, More Friends of Jesus and Recent Friends of Jesus* by Victoria Hummell, McCrimmons.)
- God's Story 3.
- Picture of a rainbow or a striped scarf etc.
- Pictures of the country where the families, of some of the children, may have come from.
- Church's Story 3, pp.33-35.
- Blank cards and envelopes.
- Some of the Beatitudes written out on a card.

This is what you are trying to communicate

Difference is a gift and sometimes a challenge. The Church family is worldwide; it is found all over the world in different countries and cultures. Saints came from all over the world and each of them were different. They help us to see we all belong to the family of God.

How we might go about it

Welcome and gathering

Have a short moment of stillness, with some music or a bell. Whilst the candle is being lit, make the Sign of the Cross. Invite the children to look at the map of the world and the display of pictures thinking about the different places they come from. Although we are all different each one is special, made and loved by God. Together we belong to his family.

Listen to the words of Psalm 100:1-5 from God's Story 3, p.52. Invite the children to repeat the response: *'Come everyone sing to God.'*

Let's remember

Ask the children to remember the last session, share/discuss the page in the workbook from the previous session. They may recall:

* Who our neighbours are.
* Something about the story of the Good Samaritan and what Jesus said about being a neighbour.

Let's share

Look at the picture of a rainbow.

Some questions to wonder about

* What do you see? How is the rainbow/scarf enhanced by the different colours?
* What would life be like if there were no colours?
* Think of different varieties animals and plants there are. How do they enhance our life?
* Think about how everyone is different. None of us are the same. Think about the differences that there are e.g. colour of eyes, interests, personality, taste in music, in food, in clothes.
* How are you different from your brothers and sisters or friends?
* What do you think about difference?

Let's discover

Difference is amazing and wonderful. All the different people, plants, animals, seasons and scenery within creation are good and show us more about God our Creator who made them all so varied and different. God also gave us many different personal qualities. Recall the very first session, where we thought about *'qualities'* (see p 21). We started this book by being amazed at God's gifts to us. God gives each one dignity. Jesus says *'I Call You Friends'*. As his friends, we are all called to be saints (holy people, friends of Jesus). We are saints in the making. What are saints like? They are all different.

Some questions to wonder about

* Why do you think saints are important?
* Is anyone in the group named after a saint?
* Do we know any other saints?

Jesus gives us some guidance about how to live as his friends. Listen to his 'way of living' by reading from God's Story 3, p.82 (based on Matthew 5:1-17). Give out cards with the Beatitudes written on them and invite some of the children to read them, pausing between each.

* Which 'way of living' (Beatitudes) did you like best and why?
* What would that mean for you in every day life?

Activities

Activity A

Use Widgit symbol simple versions of the lives of the saints with appropriate multi-sensory/inter-active props, encouraging child to choose favourite story/person.

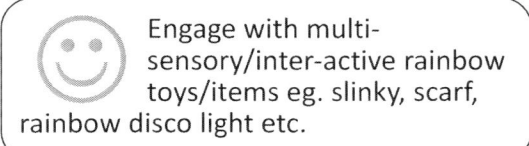

Engage with multi-sensory/inter-active rainbow toys/items eg. slinky, scarf, rainbow disco light etc.

❖ Find out about a saint who followed Jesus' 'way of living' (Beatitudes). In small groups read about the life of a saint. Each group in turn could share what they have found out about the life of the saint and think about how each saint is different. What can we learn from them?

Continued ▷

Activities continued

Activity B

❖ Ask the children if they know of any modern day people who follow Jesus' way; living or dead. Why are/were they good people? What can we learn from them? Share how saints challenge us and how they help us to see that we all belong to the family of God.

Activity book

Give out the blank cards and ask the children to make an invitation card for the Reflect and connect at the end of the last session, talk about who they might like to invite.

Talk about how you will be ending the final session, ask for ideas for prayers, hymns for the Reflect and connect. Talk about the party afterwards.

Reflect and connect

Gather round the prayer focus. Thank God for all the people who are trying to make our world a better place. Invite the children to offer their prayers for places around the world where this is happening.

Finish by reading Colossians 3:10-11, (God's Story 3, p.147).

Sing: '*He's got the whole world in his hands*', (ICYF-CD1 / AYOC 22).

Leader's Book 2 Summer Theme 9 | Session 27 | 79

SESSION 27:
Outreach
The work of the worldwide Christian family

Before you begin

Reflect on what this means to you:

'The Spirit of the Lord is upon me, because he has chosen me to bring good news to the poor.'

Luke 4:18

From the Catechism of the Catholic Church, 1825:
'The Lord ask us to love as he does... to make ourselves the neighbour of those furthest away, and to love children and the poor as Christ himself.'

This is what you are trying to communicate

As Christians we believe that everyone is made in the likeness of God and therefore we are called to care for the poor and those who are suffering injustice wherever they are.

You will need
- PRAYER FOCUS with: a collage showing images of suffering and injustice in the world, with the heading *'Make a Difference'*.
- The Good News Bible.
- Church's Story 3 and God's Story 3. (The following websites may help: www.cafod.org.uk (CAFOD Primary) and www.mission.org.uk (Missio).
- Certificates. You might give out the certificates today or at next the Sunday Mass after the end of the programme.
- Refreshments.

How we might go about it

Welcome and gathering

Have a short moment of stillness, with some music or a bell. Whilst the candle is being lit, make the Sign of the Cross.

Invite the children to gather around the collage and spend a few moments in prayer for each situation of need they see. Read: *'Go out all over the world'* from God's Story 3, p.130 (based on Matthew 28:18-20 or read from the Good News Bible.

Sing an appropriate song such as: *'Will you come and follow me?'*, (ICYF-CD4 / CFE 812).

Let's remember

Ask the children to remember the last session, share/discuss the page in the workbook from the previous session. They may recall:

* How we are all different
* Some of the saints who were mentioned.
* How the saints help us to be better friends of Jesus.

Let's share

Remember the session we shared on neighbours, how going out to others makes a difference to others and to ourselves.

Some questions to wonder about

* Can you talk about a time when you helped someone in need?
* Why did you help them?
* How did you feel afterwards?
* How has anyone ever helped you?
* What difference did it make to you?

Let's discover

When we baptised we were asked to share the light of Christ with others, to spread the Good News of God's love. We are all disciples of Jesus.

Read: 'Tell the Good News' from Church's Story 3, p.20. Jesus tried to explain that whatever good we do to others we really do it him: Matthew 25:35-45, God's Story 3, p.88 starting at 'When I was hungry...'

Some questions to wonder about

* How do you think the word 'outreach' is connected to this reading?
* How do you think you bring Good News to these people?
* Do you think our good deeds show God's love for all of us?

We can do some things alone but we can achieve much more when working with other people for a common purpose.

Activity

A. Take one of the actions Jesus spoke about and explain to a partner how you could outreach to someone in this situation today. e.g. who is a stranger today? Who is hungry etc. Use CAFOD resources.

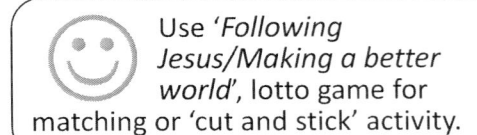

Use 'Following Jesus/Making a better world', lotto game for matching or 'cut and stick' activity.

B. Use CAFOD resources: in groups interview a local CAFOD representative trying to discover how we as a country can help others.

Activity book

Talk about the page in the Activity book.

Reflect and connect

(Invite the parents/carers and the parish priest to this final gathering and make it a ritual of celebration and joy.)

Gather round the prayer focus. In this final time together, play some quiet music, whilst everyone thinks quietly about what they have experienced during their sessions of *I Call Your Friends*. Then invite each child to come and put their Activity book on the prayer focus and say what has been important to them (including the leader).

Have a few moments of stillness.

Use the ideas of the children for the hymn and prayers. (e.g. spontaneous prayers for all those who have participated and helped in the sessions.

Say together 'Glory be to the Father...'

Sing the group's favourite hymn.

Finish by saying the words we hear each Sunday at the end of Mass: *'Go in peace to love and serve the Lord. Amen'*.

Give everyone a round of applause.

HAVE A PARTY TO CELEBRATE!

Points to remember

Check food allergies and make sure everyone has someone to invite.

Resources

Essential resources

📖 Books — *Publisher's Ref.*

The following National Project publications may be obtained from McCrimmons (www.mccrimmons.com):

- GOD'S STORY 2 — 1 899481 17 6
- GOD'S STORY 3 — 1 899481 18 4
- CHURCH'S STORY 2 — 1 899481 23 0
- CHURCH'S STORY 3 — 1 899481 24 9

📖 Other books — *Publisher's Ref.*

- CATHOLIC GOOD NEWS BIBLE — 978-0-00-720270-6

💿 CDs — *Publisher's Ref.*

- GOD'S STORY CD — 1 899481 20 6
- CHURCH'S STORY CD — 1 899481 25 7

💿 Music CDs — *Publisher's Ref.*

- I CALL YOU FRIENDS — ICYF-CD
  Music to accompany the series. Four CD set. (www.mccrimmons.com)

Additional recommended resources

📖 Stories

- FRIENDS OF JESUS. Victoria Hummell, McCrimmons. ISBN: 978-085597-640-8
- MORE FRIENDS OF JESUS. Victoria Hummell, McCrimmons. ISBN: 978-085597-650-0
- RECENT FRIENDS OF JESUS. Victoria Hummell, McCrimmons. ISBN: 978-085597-667-5

👁 Multimedia

- IMFH's FRIENDS, IMFH Publications. 1 South Hill, Upton Grey, Hampshire, RG25 2SH / www.imfhpublications.com

💿 Music CDs

- I CALL YOU FRIENDS: Music to accompany the series. Four CD set. McCrimmons: ICYF-CD
- SHARE THE LIGHT CDs: Bernadette Farrell. Signing for all the songs is on a CD-ROM with the CD. OCP Publications: ISBN 68371 11512

Key to hymn and song book references

All titles are available from McCrimmons.
www.mccrimmons.com / sales@mccrimmons.com

ICYF-CD	=	I Call You Friends CD (1, 2, 3, 4) (One collection of 4 CDs)
AYOC	=	A Year of Celebration
CFE	=	Celebration Hymnal for Everyone
P&P2	=	Project & Play 2 (Piano)

☺ Special needs resources

- Widgit Resources have some symbol-supported text which could be used for such things as lotto games, where the children match the pictures and talk about them. *A child's book of signed prayers:* Cath Smith available from Catholic Deaf Association. Simple prayers using British Sign Language, see website www.britishsignlanguage.com
- CONNECTING WITH RE, Liz O'Brien (RE and faith development for children with autism and/or severe and complex learning disabilities). Church House Publishing, 2002, ISBN 978 0 7151 4984 3.
- SPECIAL CHILDREN, SPECIAL NEEDS (integrating children with disabilities and special needs into your church), Simon Bass, Church House Publishing, 2003, ISBN 0 7151 4999 7
- TOP TIPS ON WELCOMING SPECIAL CHILDREN, Denise Abrahall (practical pointers for anyone working with children) published by Scripture Union, 2005, ISBN 1 84427 126 9.
- CD's, DVD's and song sheets with symbols from PROSPECTS (formerly Causeway), PO Box 351, Reading, Berkshire, RG1 7AL, Tel. 0118 950 8781, Email: info@prospects.org.uk

For leaders, parents, carers to use with children

- *Welcome to the Mass:* Pauline Books and Media resource: A3 photo book for display; CD-Rom and teaching notes. Code 17201
- *Praying with children,* Jenny Pate, McCrimmon Publishing Company Ltd, ISBN 0 85597 546 6
- *The Lord be with you:* introducing the Mass to children, Jenny Pate, McCrimmon Publishing Company Ltd, ISBN 0 85597 579 2
- Lion Books and Candle Books produce excellent publications.

Websites

LENT AND EASTER CALENDARS

- Calendars are usually available from:
    www.missio.org.uk
    www.mccrimmons.com

- CAFOD produce a number of resources, on the primary section of their website, which can be useful:
    www.cafod.org.uk

WIDGET SYMBOLS
www.widgit.com

MCCRIMMON PUBLISHING CO., LTD.
www.mccrimmons.com

Some useful prayers

The Our Father

*Our Father who art in Heaven
   hallowed be thy name.
Thy kingdom come,
   thy will be done on earth*

*as it is in Heaven.
Give us this day our daily bread
   and forgive us our trespasses
   as we forgive those
   who trespass against us,
   and deliver us from evil.*

Amen.

The Hail Mary

*Hail Mary full of grace
   the Lord is with thee.
Blessed art thou among women and
   blessed is the fruit of thy womb
   Jesus.*

*Holy Mary Mother of God
   pray for us sinners
   now and at the hour of our death.*

Amen.

A sorry prayer

*God, Our Father,
   thank you for loving me.*

*I am sorry for the times
   I have not loved others or you.*

Help me to always live as Jesus lived.

Amen.

Glory be to the Father

*Glory be to the Father
   and to the Son
   and to the Holy Spirit,
as it was in the beginning
   is now and ever shall be
   world without end.*

Amen.

A morning prayer

*Dear God,
thank you for the morning,
   bless us all today.*

*Be with me as I work and play
   and help me love you more
   and more.*

Amen.

Health and Safety

Every parish will have guidelines on health and safety which need to be known and followed. As leader, it is your responsibility to ensure that the place where you are meeting is safe.

* Take care when lighting candles, it is better to light the candle for prayer and extinguish it when the prayer has ended.
* Check any significant health issues. Check with the parents whether any child has allergies.
* Make sure the place you are meeting is clean and has nothing in it that children could trip on. If you are using a CD player or power point be careful of leads.
* Check the toilets are usable and that they have paper and washing facilities.
* If you have children with special needs, ensure with the parents that you know about the child's needs.

Safeguarding Children

It is important for the welfare of the children in your care and for your own protection that you have a copy and are familiar with the parish/diocesan guidelines for safeguarding children. It will be helpful to know who the parish representative for Safeguarding is. Everyone involved with the children will need a current CRB (Criminal Records Bureau) check. This is normally done through the diocese before the catechist or any helpers have contact with the children.

The following offer some ideas but where it is different from your own parish policy, it is essential that you following the parish guidelines.

1. Ensure that a minimum of two leaders/workers are always present. In groups of more than 20 there should be one additional helper for every 10 children.
2. With activities away from the normal meeting place, the ratio should be 1:7.
3. With children under 8 years old the recommended ratio is 1:6.
4. Never let a child wander out of the meeting room unsupervised.
5. When children are being picked up at the end of the session, ensure you know who it is who will collect them. Never allow a child to depart with a stranger.
6. If you are taking photographs of children, ensure you have written permission from the parents.
7. If you are displaying photos of the children in the church ensure the children are not named and that you have the parents' permission to display the photographs.
8. Leaders need to understand and avoid situations of potential danger or embarrassment, for example, being one to one in private with a child, or driving a child home in a car.
9. Ensure that leaders know what to do in the case of suspected or alleged abuse.
10. Ensure there is adequate insurance cover, especially for activities away from the normal meeting place.
11. Activities away from the normal meeting place require a consent form signed by the parents or guardians. Information would also be required concerning any special medical prescription, for example inhalers.
12. Keep a register of up-to-date information: name of the child, address, telephone number, special medications, the name, address and phone number of the child's doctor and a signed permission form from the parents or guardians for the leader to be in loco parentis in case of emergency.
13. Keep an attendance register for the sessions.
14. Ensure the premises used are safe, well maintained and be familiar with fire precaution and apparatus.
15. Ensure there is a first aid kit and that it is checked frequently.
16. Ensure that at least one adult has a mobile phone with them in working order and in case of being out of range there is a need to be aware of where the nearest public telephone is for emergencies.
17. Ensure that someone knows where the group is and who is in the group, if the group is working away from the normal meeting place. It is necessary that the group reports out and back.
18. Ensure that where vehicles are used there is adequate insurance and permits, that seat belts and any other special equipment are properly maintained, for example, wheelchair access lifts.
19. Accidents/incidents must be recorded with the date, time and names.

You must...

a. Treat all children with respect.
b. Provide an example of good conduct that you wish others to follow.
c. Be aware that even caring physical contact with a child may be misinterpreted.
d. Show understanding when dealing with sensitive issues.

Notes

Notes

Notes